Cyberbullying

Peggy J. Parks

The Internet

ReferencePoint
Press®

San Diego, CA

© 2013 ReferencePoint Press, Inc.
Printed in the United States

For more information, contact:
ReferencePoint Press, Inc.
PO Box 27779
San Diego, CA 92198
www.ReferencePointPress.com

Picture credits:
Cover: Thinkstock/iStockphoto
Maury Aaseng: 31–33, 45–47, 59–60, 72–74
© Najlah Feanny/Corbis: 17
Thinkstock/Goodshoot: 10

LIBRARY OF CONGRESS CATALOGING-IN-PUBLICATION DATA

Parks, Peggy J., 1951–
    Cyberbullying / by Peggy J. Parks.
        p. cm. -- (Compact research)
    Includes bibliographical references and index.
    ISBN-13: 978-1-60152-262-7 (hardback)
    ISBN-10: 1-60152-262-2 (hardback)
 1. Cyberbullying--Juvenile literature. I. Title.
    HV6773.15.C92P37   2012
    302.34'3--dc23

                                                        2011047780

Contents

Foreword

As modern civilization continues to evolve, its ability to create, store, distribute, and access information expands exponentially. The explosion of information from all media continues to increase at a phenomenal rate. By 2020 some experts predict the worldwide information base will double every 73 days. While access to diverse sources of information and perspectives is paramount to any democratic society, information alone cannot help people gain knowledge and understanding. Information must be organized and presented clearly and succinctly in order to be understood. The challenge in the digital age becomes not the creation of information, but how best to sort, organize, enhance, and present information.

ReferencePoint Press developed the *Compact Research* series with this challenge of the information age in mind. More than any other subject area today, researching current issues can yield vast, diverse, and unqualified information that can be intimidating and overwhelming for even the most advanced and motivated researcher. The *Compact Research* series offers a compact, relevant, intelligent, and conveniently organized collection of information covering a variety of current topics ranging from illegal immigration and deforestation to diseases such as anorexia and meningitis.

The series focuses on three types of information: objective single-author narratives, opinion-based primary source quotations, and facts and statistics. The clearly written objective narratives provide context and reliable background information. Primary source quotes are carefully selected and cited, exposing the reader to differing points of view, and facts and statistics sections aid the reader in evaluating perspectives. Presenting these key types of information creates a richer, more balanced learning experience.

For better understanding and convenience, the series enhances information by organizing it into narrower topics and adding design features that make it easy for a reader to identify desired content. For example, in *Compact Research: Illegal Immigration*, a chapter covering the economic impact of illegal immigration has an objective narrative explaining the various ways the economy is impacted, a balanced section of numerous primary source quotes on the topic, followed by facts and full-color illustrations to encourage evaluation of contrasting perspectives.

The ancient Roman philosopher Lucius Annaeus Seneca wrote, "It is quality rather than quantity that matters." More than just a collection of content, the *Compact Research* series is simply committed to creating, finding, organizing, and presenting the most relevant and appropriate amount of information on a current topic in a user-friendly style that invites, intrigues, and fosters understanding.

Cyberbullying at a Glance

Cyberbullying Defined

Any bullying behavior (such as harassment) that involves the Internet or cell phones is considered cyberbullying.

Bullying Versus Cyberbullying

Many experts say that cyberbullying is worse than traditional bullying because of anonymity, a victim's inability to escape from the abuse, and the vast size of the potential audience.

Cyberbullying Tactics

Cyberbullies harass their victims with abusive text messages, impersonate them by creating fake pages on social networking sites, and degrade them with online postings that can ruin their reputations.

Prevalence

Surveys have shown that about one out of five youths between the ages of 10 and 18 have been either a perpetrator of cyberbullying or a victim. Gay, lesbian, bisexual, and transgender youth have a markedly higher risk of being cyberbullied.

Warning Signs

Kids who are cyberbullied often display changes in personality such as being withdrawn and moody rather than outgoing and social, do not want to go to school, and become agitated after being online or checking text messages.

Consequences

Victims of cyberbullying have higher-than-normal incidences of depression, poor self-esteem, and suicidal thoughts.

Legislation

As of November 2011, 35 states had enacted antibullying legislation that includes electronic harassment and/or cyberbullying.

First Amendment Issues

Cyberbullying laws are often challenged because the US Constitution guarantees freedom of speech, and laws that limit it could be unconstitutional.

Prevention

Because cyberbullying is so widespread and most commonly affects adolescents, it is difficult to stop. Tactics that have been effective include education and awareness efforts, peer-to-peer programs, and presentations at schools by people who have lost family members due to bullying-related suicides.

Overview

After winning a long, painful battle against cancer, all Justine Williams wanted was for her life to get back to normal. Diagnosed with bone cancer at the age of 10, she underwent grueling bouts of chemotherapy, lost all her hair, and had to have her left leg amputated. Just before her fourteenth birthday she was fitted with a prosthetic leg, and with the help of a physical therapist she learned how to walk again. When she started the eighth grade during the fall of 2010, Williams thought that her nightmare was finally over—but a few months later a new nightmare began with a vicious cyberbullying attack.

At first the contact seemed innocent enough, with text messages telling Williams to have a good day at school. But then the tone changed drastically. Not only did the texts become more frequent, they got progressively nastier and more threatening, saying that a bomb had been planted outside Williams's house, that she was going to be raped, and that her pets were going to be killed. Even though Williams was frightened and did not want to go to school, at first she told no one. Finally she confessed to her older sister and then to her parents, who called the police. The cyberbully was caught, and although Williams was relieved to hear that, she was hurt and confused about what was done to her. She explains: "I couldn't believe someone would do that because I've already been through enough as it is and I didn't see why someone had to put more stress into my life."[1] Williams was also disheartened to learn that the girl who had been bullying her was her best friend—or rather, someone she *thought* was her best friend.

Abuse of Technology

It is an unfortunate fact that bullying has always existed in one form or another. Young people are often told by their parents, and also their grandparents, that dealing with bullies is just part of being a kid. Although this may be true to some extent, cyberbullying is different in ways that were completely unknown to previous generations. Psychologist Marie Hartwell-Walker writes: "As harmful as bullying has always been, what many adults don't seem to understand is that it's moved to a dangerously different level now."[2]

Cyberbullying is defined as any harassment that occurs via the Internet or digital communication. This includes e-mail, instant messages, comments on social networking sites such as Facebook, posts on other websites or blogs, and videos posted on YouTube. With the exploding popularity of cell phone text messaging, cyberbullies can also harass their victims by sending them abusive text messages.

> " Because of the worldwide reach of the Internet and digital technology, the ability of cyberbullies to abuse their victims is virtually limitless. "

In surveys, young people say they view cyberbullying as a serious problem. Abusive text messages and postings on social networking sites are the dominant forms of cyberbullying among teenagers.

How *Cyber* Has Changed *Bullying*

Cyberbullying is different from face-to-face bullying in a number of ways, one of which is the vast size of the audience. In the past, a bully's taunts were confined to a specific area such as a school or playground, but that is no longer the case. Because of the worldwide reach of the Internet and digital technology, the ability of cyberbullies to abuse their victims is virtually limitless. Says George C. Venizelos, an agent with the Philadelphia division of the Federal Bureau of Investigation (FBI): "We cannot . . . underestimate the impact of bullying when it is enhanced by cyber means. Gone are the days of the proverbial 'playground bully,' as that playground has now expanded exponentially via the Internet. The relative perceived anonymity of the Internet appears to empower individuals to say and do things they would not do in person."[3]

Venizelos's reference to anonymity exemplifies another way that technology has changed bullying. People can set up e-mail addresses by using pseudonyms rather than their real names and then post abusive messages on social networking sites or in online forums, or harass via e-mail, without anyone knowing who they are. For many who are cyberbullied, this can be worse than face-to-face bullying and cause a great deal of stress. As one teenager from Illinois told the Cyberbullying Research Center: "I get mean messages on Formspring, with people telling me I'm fat and ugly and stupid. I don't know what I ever did to anyone. I wish it wasn't anonymous."[4]

> " Harassment involves the continuous badgering of someone with offensive, insulting, or threatening messages through instant messaging, e-mail, or cell phone texting. "

Also unique to cyberbullying is accessibility. With face-to-face bullying, someone who is away from school on weekends or during vacations can often escape from the harassment. With cyberbullying, however, victims cannot escape—it can follow them wherever they go, any time of the day or night, every day of the week. Los Angeles attorney Millie Anne Cavanaugh writes:

With cyberbullying, the torment does not stop when the bell rings. With the advent of the Internet, bullies can now torment, threaten, harass, humiliate, and embarrass their classmates at night, and on the weekends too. . . . Where before rumors and hate were spread by passing notes or creating "slam" books, bullies can now deliver daily doses of humiliation by simply posting a message on their personal web page or sending an e-mail about the victim to everyone in the class.[5]

Cyberbullying Tactics

The methods that cyberbullies use to taunt and torment their victims differ on the basis of the people involved and the types of media used. Harassment, for instance, involves the continuous badgering of someone with offensive, insulting, and/or threatening messages through instant messaging, e-mail, or cell phone texting. An example of this type of cyberbullying is what happened to Justine Williams, who received over 90 text messages that got progressively nastier and more threatening as time went by.

Another tactic used by cyberbullies is denigration, which involves degrading someone in an effort to damage his or her reputation and friendships. For example, someone might set up a social networking site that is intended to make fun of or embarrass another person. The creator of this site typically will call on others to post photographs, negative comments, rumors, and gossip about that person. Nancy Willard, who is the executive director of the Center for Safe and Responsible Use of the Internet, refers to this type of cyberbullying as "dissing" someone online. She writes: "Some boys created a 'We Hate Joe' Web site where they posted jokes, cartoons, gossip, and rumors, all dissing Joe."[6]

When asked about cyberbullying in surveys, most young people say that it is a serious problem for kids their age.

David Knight, a teenager from Canada, was the target of this sort of cyberbullying. He had long been the victim of face-to-face bullying at school, and he went through a difficult time because of it. But when he found out that some of his classmates had launched an abusive website specifically targeted at him, he found the humiliation unbearable. Knight did not know about the site until a boy at school told him about it. When he went online to look at the site, he found his photograph and the greeting "Welcome to the Web Site that makes fun of Dave Knight" along with an invitation for others to join in and post negative comments. Knight was devastated to see what people were saying about him, which he says included "just pages of hateful comments directed at me and everyone in my family."[7]

How Serious a Problem Is Cyberbullying?

Internet security experts widely agree that cyberbullying is a pervasive problem. According to a 2010 survey by the Cyberbullying Research Center, one in five youths between the ages of 10 and 18 have either been a victim of cyberbullying or have participated in it themselves. Other studies show even greater prevalence, such as one conducted by Crisp Thinking, a United Kingdom–based firm that helps businesses protect youth from online bullies. The group says that cyberbullying is an enormous threat to kids, affecting an estimated one-third of those who are online. Attorney and cybersecurity expert Parry Aftab says that not only is cyberbullying a serious problem—it is a problem that is growing worse, as she explains: "We are seeing cyberbullying happening at broader age ranges and for longer periods of time. It's exploding."[8]

When asked about cyberbullying in surveys, most young people say that it is a serious problem for kids their age. That was the view of over 75 percent of participants in an August 2011 survey of teens and young adults by MTV and the Associated Press. The survey also revealed that 56 percent of participants had personally experienced cyber abuse, which was an increase of 6 percent over a 2009 survey by the same group. An encouraging finding, though, was that compared with the 2009 survey, a significantly higher number of participants said they were likely to intervene if they noticed someone being mean online.

Kids in Pain

It is not uncommon for young people who are cyberbullied to keep what is happening to themselves rather than tell their parents or other trusted adults. This is often because they fear that by telling someone they will be perceived as a "snitch," which will make the harassment worse. Another reason cyberbullying victims often keep silent is that they do not want to risk having their parents curtail their Internet privileges or take away their cell phones. Olweus, a bullying prevention program, states: "Often, adults' responses to cyber bullying are to remove the technology from a victim—which in their eyes can be seen as punishment."[9] But even if cyberbullying victims do not let anyone know, those who are closest to them can usually tell that something is wrong.

> One of the most obvious signs that someone is being cyberbullied is a distinct change in personality.

One of the most obvious signs that someone is being cyberbullied is a distinct change in personality. For instance, if a person who was formerly outgoing and social suddenly becomes withdrawn, moody, and anxious, this could be a warning sign. Minneapolis attorney Arthur Kosieradzki writes: "If the child or teen hates going out, or finds excuses to stay home, especially from activities involving peers, it can be cause for concern. Cyberbullying can make a child tense, tearful, and defensive, and cause a sudden loss of interest in favorite activities."[10] Cyberbullying experts say that another symptom is when a young person seems upset or angry after being online or checking cell phone text messages.

Why People Cyberbully

Psychologists and Internet security experts have extensively studied cyberbullying, with one focus on determining why people engage in it. Surveys of students in middle school and high school have consistently shown that those who participate in cyberbullying do so for multiple reasons. Aftab explains: "When it comes to cyberbullying, they are often motivated by anger, revenge or frustration. Sometimes they do it for entertainment or because they are bored and have too much time on their hands and too many tech toys available to them. Many do it for laughs or to get a reaction."[11]

For a study published in August 2010, researchers from Georgia State University sought high school students' perceptions about motivations of cyberbullies. Some of the reasons given included wanting to appear tougher or cooler online than they were in real life, boredom, jealousy, and a desire to gain attention and/or acceptance from their peers. Respondents also said that some who cyberbully do so out of revenge; it was the only way they felt they could get back at people who had hurt them. As one student who admitted to cyberbullying a classmate said: "I was really angry and he was not nice to me and he deserved it."[12]

What Are the Consequences of Cyberbullying?

The Internet and digital communication offer would-be bullies the unprecedented ability to torment their victims, and this can be traumatic for those on the receiving end of the abuse. Teen surveys have shown that victims of cyberbullying often suffer from low self-esteem, poor grades in school, insecurity, and inability to feel safe in their own homes. Says Steven Goldstein, who is chairman of the New Jersey gay rights organization Garden State Equality: "Cyberbullying doesn't give students an opportunity to heal and move on because there is always the threat that the harassing email can be forwarded to thousands of additional people at the touch of a keyboard. How horrifying is that?"[13]

Cyberbullying can indeed be horrifying for those who are targeted by it, even demoralizing them to the point of feeling totally defeated. This is what happened to Taylor Riberio, a teenager from Meriden, Connecticut. In just one year, Riberio changed from a happy, outgoing girl who loved sports to someone who was depressed and withdrawn and who had lost interest in everything she once enjoyed. When she started her freshman year of high school, Riberio started hanging out with a new group of friends who were known for being a bit wild. She wanted them to accept her, so when they bullied other kids, she joined in. She soon realized, however, that she wanted no part of it and tried to leave the group—which was when her nightmare began.

> **One of the most contentious issues related to cyberbullying is whether legislation is the answer to stopping it.**

Now considered an outcast, Riberio was taunted by vicious instant messages whenever she got online. She also found that Facebook pages had been created with titles such as "People Who Think Taylor Riberio Should Die" and "People Who Think Taylor Riberio's Family Should Die." Her mother, Lynn Ryder, knew something was terribly wrong when Riberio's personality changed and she started skipping school, but the girl would not say what was going on. After she disappeared for a few days, Ryder called the police, and they found her daughter. Riberio was diagnosed with depression and admitted to a psychiatric facility, where she finally opened up to a counselor about what had been done to her. After months of therapy, she returned home determined to fight back if she is ever cyberbullied again. She explains: "Everyone is going to remember not a girl who hung out with cyber bullies, but a girl who got cyber bullied and got her life back."[14]

The Link Between Cyberbullying and Suicide

Because of widespread publicity over the tragic suicides of teens who were bullied, awareness of the harmful effects of bullying has soared in recent years. This has given rise to the term "bullycide," which implies that someone was "bullied to death." Hartwell-Walker writes: "What only a generation ago took days to get around school, now can take minutes. There's little time to confront a rumor, to clarify a remark, or to stand up to a bully when negative messages get so widespread so fast and when the bully is able to be anonymous. . . . Tragically, this is leading to increasing numbers of suicides among our teens."[15]

> **Despite the challenges, increased public awareness of the harm caused by cyberbullying has sparked a number of efforts on the part of schools, parent groups, and state legislatures.**

While some people see a clear connection between bullying and suicide, there often is no way to know if bullying *caused* someone to take his or her own life or if other problems triggered such action. The perspective of Paul Butler, a former federal prosecutor who is now associate dean and a law professor at the George Washington University Law School, is that suicide is a tragic response to bullying but an uncommon one. He writes: "Of the millions of children who

Various efforts are under way to stop cyberbullying. These include new laws; awareness campaigns, which promote bully-free zones; peer-to-peer programs; and school presentations by family members of young people who committed suicide after experiencing cyberbullying.

suffer bullying, few take their own lives. Bullies 'cause' suicides in the same way that a man 'causes' the suicide of a lover he spurns."[16]

Are More Stringent Cyberbullying Laws Needed?

One of the most contentious issues related to cyberbullying is whether legislation is the answer to stopping it. Those who are against such laws offer a number of reasons for their objections, such as their concern that legislation could potentially violate people's constitutional right to free speech. Other objections include the belief that existing laws could deter cyberbullying if they were more stringently enforced, and that the best solution to putting an end to cyberbullying is education and awareness rather than more laws.

Advocates of cyberbullying laws agree that education and awareness programs are valuable and necessary. They argue, however, that such tactics alone are not enough; that tougher measures are necessary in order to get the message across that cyberbullying will not be tolerated. In a September 2011 report, four New York state senators who compose the Independent Democratic Conference write: "All the driver's ed classes in the world have not stopped reckless driving, and awareness training alone won't put an end to cyberbullying either. The key is to tackle the problem from all sides." By "all sides," the group is referring to combining awareness and education with cyberbullying laws, the latter of which members say is a "way of incentivizing bullies to refrain from online harassment while providing the tools for prosecution if they don't."[17] A growing number of state legislators agree with this perspective and are acting accordingly. As of November 2011, 35 states had enacted antibullying legislation that includes electronic harassment, with 10 of those states specifically using the term *cyberbullying*.

Can Cyberbullying Be Prevented?

Trying to stop cyberbullying is a difficult, and some say impossible, feat for a number of reasons. A major hurdle is tracking down cyberbullies in the worldwide maze of the Internet and digital communications, and another is the ease of taunting and abusing victims behind a shield of anonymity. Despite the challenges, increased public awareness of the harm caused by cyberbullying has sparked a number of efforts on the part of schools, parent groups, and state legislatures. For instance, education targeted at children and teens has been shown to make a positive difference in preventing cyberbullying, as Aftab explains: "We need to address ways they can become inadvertent cyberbullies, how to be accountable for their actions and not to stand by and allow bullying (in any form) to be acceptable. We need to teach them not to ignore the pain of others."[18]

One program that is proving to be successful at preventing cyberbullying is called Safe School Ambassadors (SSA), which is for students in fourth through twelfth grades. Its creator, Rick Phillips, is executive director and founder of the group Community Matters. He describes the program as "the power of the few to influence the many." Student leaders are identified and selected as facilitators and then trained in problem-solving and intervention techniques that help resolve bullying issues before they escalate. Says Phillips: "When young people are engaged, equipped, and empowered to speak up, bullying decreases and school climate improves. . . . This is the social vaccine and approach that can prevent and eradicate the acts of cruelty and electronic harassment that we all want to see stopped."[19]

A Disturbing Problem

Like traditional bullying, cyberbullying involves abusive behavior toward someone who, for whatever reason, is chosen as a target—but there are also important differences. Cyberbullies may avail themselves of the broad reach of the Internet and cell phone technology, which gives them virtually unlimited exposure and anonymity. To help resolve the problem, cybersecurity experts, parent groups, and educators are developing solutions designed to spread awareness of cyberbullying and put a stop to it. Hopefully these efforts will result in fewer people having to suffer from harassment and abuse.

How Serious a Problem Is Cyberbullying?

❝Being a kid is hard enough without having to go through the torture of being cyberbullied.❞

—Rob Frappier, community manager for Reputation.com, a business specializing in personal privacy and online reputation management services.

❝An increasing number of youth are misusing online technology—e-mailing, text messaging, chatting and blogging—to bully, harass and even incite violence against others.❞

—Anti-Defamation League, which fights bigotry in the United States and abroad through education, legislation, and advocacy.

On June 24, 2010, Phillip C. McGraw testified at a US House of Representatives hearing on student cyber safety. A psychologist best known for hosting the *Dr. Phil* daytime television program, McGraw referred to cyberbullying as a "serious crisis" affecting youth. "In the past," he said, "a bully had physical size and words. Now the cyber-bully has Facebook, MySpace, Email, Texting, Web Postings, blocked calling via the Internet, Instant Messaging, and chat rooms." McGraw emphasized that because of this technology, cyberbullies today have the unprecedented capability of causing pain and suffering to their victims: "In a matter of seconds, a cyber-bully can completely destroy a fragile adolescent's reputation. While a bully's rumors in the 1980s might have reached twenty people, a cyber-bully's rumors will reach millions. . . . And what makes it worse for these victims is that there is absolutely no place for them to hide."[20]

No Way to Escape

The fact that there is no escape from a cyberbully's abuse is a major reason why cyberbullying is often called the worst form of bullying. The taunting is always there, mocking victims anytime they log into Facebook, open up their e-mails, or turn on their cell phones. To live with that kind of fear and dread day after day can wear a person down, making him or her feel powerless as well as hopeless. Joseph D. Early Jr. witnessed this with an 11-year old boy who had been viciously cyberbullied. Early, who is the district attorney in Worcester, Massachusetts, says he was heartbroken when he heard the boy say he would rather be physically beaten than face constant humiliation online or through text messages. "For some kids it's just totally debilitating," says Early. "They wake up in the morning just dreading what they're going to see online. They don't want to go to school, they don't want to turn on the computer."[21]

A report presented at the American Psychological Association's annual convention in August 2011 reinforced the view that cyberbullying can be more traumatic than being harassed in person. The presenters, including psychologist Elizabeth Carll, stated that victims experience high levels of stress, anxiety, shock, and fear, as well as feelings of helplessness. Many also suffer from sleeping problems and are plagued by nightmares. Carll is convinced that the symptoms related to cyberbullying can be more difficult to bear than in-person harassment, as she explains: "The impact is more devastating due to the 24/7 nature of online communication, inability to escape to a safe place, and global access of the information."[22]

> " The fact that there is no escape from a cyberbully's abuse is a major reason why cyberbullying is often called the worst form of bullying. "

A teenager named Jason from Long Island, New York, understands what it feels like to be bullied, in person and online, because he has endured both. Jason has long been considered a convenient target for bullies since he is much smaller than the teenage boys who pick on him. Because of the way he chooses to dress, and the fact that his hobbies include comic books and Xbox games, his classmates call him "gay" and "loser." But even that does not hurt as much as the relentless attacks through e-mails, Facebook posts, and text messages. He explains: "It's really horrifying the next day after the message has been sent around, and you're the laughingstock of the school. You have no idea why or what's funny."[23]

Stolen Identity

Of all the ways that cyberbullies harass and torment their victims, assuming their identity is one of the most traumatic. Someone who is being impersonated, such as on a fake social networking profile created with his or her name, has no way to control what is posted, whether it is digitally altered photographs or demeaning comments. Nafeesa Onque went through this, and not only was she traumatized by the experience, her reputation was nearly shattered.

Onque is a pretty, popular teenage girl from Newark, New Jersey. In 2009 she created a Facebook page with the name Nafeesa McPomPoms Onque, with "pompoms" referring to her being a member of the high school cheerleading squad. Soon after her Facebook page was online, another one appeared with a name that was nearly identical to hers. This page, however, was filled with lewd comments, making it appear that Onque was posting about her sex life and propositioning men for sex. The imposter also pulled names from Onque's Facebook friends list and sent requests to those people and also to dozens of other teenagers. Everyone who accepted the request was bombarded with e-mails filled with nasty, profanity-laced tirades. Many contacted Onque, asking why she was sending such hateful messages to them.

As this continued Onque became fearful and withdrawn, avoiding sporting events and school dances on the weekends. "For a while I couldn't walk to the corner store by myself," she says, "or do the things I wanted to do because my parents were worried about my safety."[24] In March 2010, the situation turned dangerous. On the fake Facebook page the imposter had challenged a teenage girl to a fight, and assuming the imposter was Onque, the girl viciously attacked her in the schoolyard.

Onque and her parents had been unsuccessful at getting the Facebook page taken down and were discouraged to be told by police that there was nothing they could do. But after the physical attack they were determined to find someone who would help them. They turned to New Jersey State Police sergeant Chuck Allen of the department's Digital Technology Investigations Unit, and he agreed to investigate the case. By December 2010 he had located the cyberbully: a 15-year-old girl who attended the same school as Onque. The girl was arrested the following January and charged with wrongful impersonation.

Not Just Kid Stuff

Although most articles about cyberbullying, as well as surveys and studies, focus on children and adolescents, adults are also victimized by cyberbullies. Justin W. Patchin, who along with being codirector of the Cyberbullying Research Center also teaches criminal justice at the University of Wisconsin–Eau Claire, says that his office receives many e-mails and telephone calls from adults who have been victims of online abuse and harassment. "They stress to us that cyberbullying is not just an adolescent problem," he says. "Believe me, we know. We receive more inquiries from adults than teens. We know that cyberbullying negatively affects adults too."[25]

> Someone who is being impersonated, such as on a fake social networking profile created with his or her name, has no way to control what is posted, whether it is digitally altered photographs or demeaning comments.

Julia Allison, who is a syndicated columnist, television commentator, and news media expert, was shocked when she was targeted by cyberbullies. She thought her days of being bullied were in the distant past—but she was wrong, as she explains: "The 'in-real-life' bullying I endured in middle school was so bad that I used to come home in tears, wishing that I wouldn't wake up the next morning. And yet, here I am, more than a decade and a half later, dealing with a far more virulent strain: cyberbullying."[26]

Allison has received numerous letters and e-mails, as well as read comments online, that are filled with profanity and hatred. Most have focused on her physical appearance, as she writes: "I have body parts I didn't even know could be called hideous—'sausage fingers' and 'elephant knees,' for example. But it doesn't stop there. One commenter wrote: 'Julia, you are a despicable person. Ugly inside and out, with ZERO redeeming qualities."[27] Not only has Allison been the target of this abuse, her employer, friends, family members, and boyfriend have also been targeted.

> **Although most articles about cyberbullying, as well as surveys and studies, focus on children and adolescents, adults are also victimized by cyberbullies.**

As disturbing as this experience has been, however, Allison does not spend much time trying to understand why the cyberbullies chose her. She writes: "As a columnist and as a social media user, haters feel I am fair game. They do it because they can. Because I 'asked for it' by sharing anything at all." She emphasizes that anyone, anywhere, can be a victim of cyberbullying: "Bullying spans generations: 45-year-old bullies raise children who become 13-year-old bullies who grow up to be 28-year-old bullies. And here's my 'controversial' proposition: Kids aren't the only ones who should be protected from them."[28]

Insidious Impersonation

Susan Arnout Smith is another adult who was victimized by cyberbullies—and she was devastated over what they did to her. A writer from San Diego, Smith was alerted in 2011 by a colleague who saw a profile on Facebook with her name. She reluctantly clicked into the page, and when she saw what was posted she felt nauseous. "There are moments that are burned into the heart," she says. "I saw my face. It was a photo taken off one of my websites. I saw my name. The persona they had created, using my name, my face, was pornographic, trolling for sex. I pay good money. I sat stunned." After Smith became aware of the Facebook attack, she was so humiliated, embarrassed, and frightened of her reputation being ruined that she could not concentrate, nor could she sleep at night. Even worse, she could not write. "Writing is what I do," she says. "It's how I make my way in the world."[29]

Like so many other victims of cyberbullying, Smith had no luck in getting the page deleted from Facebook. As instructed on the site, she got into the page, clicked an icon that identified it as fake, and typed in the address for her real profile. A number of her friends, colleagues, and family members did the same, but the page remained online. "Every day, I'd click into the fake profile," she says, "hoping it was gone. Every day, it was there." As more time passed, she began to feel even more power-less and fearful. "I had built my reputation brick by brick over decades, one project at a time," she says, "only to discover that out there in cy-berspace, my life and reputation had been shredded."[30]

As discouraged as she was, Smith refused to give up, vowing to track down the impersonators on her own. After a great deal of online searching, she narrowed down their location to a country outside of the United States, and more digging yielded their city, and then the schools they attended—because, as she learned, her cy-berbullies were high school kids. Rather than attempting to have them prosecuted, she wrote to their school principals, explained what had hap-pened and how it had affected her, and demanded that the kids take the page down. Within days it was gone. In an e-mail Smith received, school officials expressed their puzzlement over why she had been targeted. "My guess?" she says. "I wasn't real to them. I was a bouncy toy, a name, a face, pulled at random off the Net. . . . That, for me, is the scariest part."[31]

> " **Cyberbullying is mean-spirited, widespread, and a serious problem.** "

"Sextbullying"

When sexually explicit photos are sent via cell phone text messaging, it is known as sexting. Sexting is not a smart thing to do; there is no way to control what happens to those photos or who will see them once they are sent. In that sense, sexting can become a tool for cyberbullies. Elizabeth C. Eraker, editor of the *Berkeley Technology Law Journal Annual Review*, says that the harmful effects of sexting are greatly compounded when it is used as a tool for online bullying. Referring to what she calls "sextbullying," Eraker writes: "Although most of the publicly reported cases of sexting involve consensual sharing between teens in a relationship, there are increasingly more examples of sext messages used as tools of coercion and harassment."[32]

A Washington girl named Margarite found herself embroiled in an embarrassing sexting incident in January 2011. The previous December, Margarite decided to sext a nude picture of herself to her new boyfriend, Isaiah. She stood naked in front of the bathroom mirror, held up her cell phone, snapped a full-length picture of herself, and sent it to his phone. Soon after that they broke up, and Isaiah forwarded the photo to a former friend of Margarite's. The girl added the text message, "Ho Alert! If you think this girl is a whore, then text this to all your friends.[33] She sent the photo and attached message to her entire list of contacts, and others forwarded it on. The photo went viral, with hundreds or perhaps even thousands of teenagers seeing it.

High-Tech Cruelty

Cyberbullying is mean-spirited, widespread, and a serious problem. Whether it involves abusive comments posted online, harassing and threatening someone by cell phone text messages, or hijacking a person's identity to create an inflammatory Facebook page, this high-tech abuse causes anguish for anyone who is unfortunate enough to be targeted by it. Says Parry Aftab: "It's not fair. It is cruel. . . . It is done as casual entertainment. And it has to stop."[34]

How Serious a Problem Is Cyberbullying?

66 Facebook and MySpace are the two leading social network sites, which have become a war zone for young adults and children in posting humiliating photos of one another, as well as inappropriate polls and language. 99

—Carl Timm and Richard Perez, *Seven Deadliest Social Network Attacks*. Burlington, MA: Syngress, 2010, p. 106.

Timm is the regional director of security services for the technology firm Savvis Communications, and Perez is the company's security and architecture practice manager.

66 Recent research studies have shown that a substantial number of students are victims of cyberbullying, which leads to a wider realization that cyberbullying is becoming a serious problem. 99

—Qing Li, "Cyberbullying in High Schools: A Study of Students' Behaviors and Beliefs About This New Phenomenon," *Journal of Aggression, Maltreatment & Trauma*, May 25, 2010. www.tandfonline.com.

Li is an associate professor of educational technology at the University of Calgary in Alberta, Canada.

* Editor's Note: While the definition of a primary source can be narrowly or broadly defined, for the purposes of Compact Research, a primary source consists of: 1) results of original research presented by an organization or researcher; 2) eyewitness accounts of events, personal experience, or work experience; 3) first-person editorials offering pundits' opinions; 4) government officials presenting political plans and/or policies; 5) representatives of organizations presenting testimony or policy.

❝It is clear that technology has made cyberbullying far worse than bullying by conventional (in person) means, as rumors may now be spread much faster to a larger number of individuals.❞

—Marie-Helen Maras, *Computer Forensics: Cybercriminals, Laws, and Evidence*. Sudbury, MA: Jones & Bartlett, 2012, p. 154.

Maras is assistant professor of criminal justice at Farmingdale State College, State University of New York.

❝There is an evolving understanding that cyber-bullying is a very serious public health problem, prevalent around the world.❞

—Jorge C. Srabstein, testimony before US House of Representatives, Committee on Education and Labor, Subcommittee on Healthy Families and Communities, "Hearing on Ensuring Student Cyber Safety," June 24, 2010. www.childrensnational.org.

Srabstein is a psychiatrist and medical director of the Clinic for Health Problems Related to Bullying at Children's National Medical Center.

❝Cyberbullying has come to the forefront of late and it needs to be addressed. Kids are cruel. Kids who take advantage of the group dynamic of the internet in order to harass another kid are downright vicious.❞

—Stan Kid, e-mail interview with author, October 11, 2010.

Kid is a lieutenant with the Malverne Police Department in Nassau County, Long Island, New York.

❝Never before has particularly cruel harassment from school persisted as long as it does now online, where for example, a Facebook group, populated with hundreds of members, is dedicated solely to making fun of a fellow classmate because of his hair color.❞

—Tom Perrelli, remarks at the US Department of Education's Bullying Summit, August 12, 2010. www.ojp.usdoj.gov.

Perrelli is the associate attorney general of the United States.

“What we know from research is that the incidence of kids harming one another psychologically in ways that are mediated by new technologies is going up over time. But those same data do not tell us that the overall incidence of bullying is going up, nor that it is getting worse.”

—John Palfrey, “Solutions Beyond the Law,” *New York Times*, October 1, 2010. www.nytimes.com.

Palfrey is a professor at Harvard Law School and the faculty codirector of the Berkman Center for Internet & Society.

“Cyberbullying, while similar to traditional harassment, does have a different quality—namely, humiliating rumors and vicious taunts can be viewed by millions online and they can never be removed from the Internet.”

—Justin W. Patchin, “Most Bullying Cases Aren't Criminal,” *New York Times*, September 30, 2010. www.nytimes.com.

Patchin is associate professor of criminal justice at the University of Wisconsin–Eau Claire and codirector of the Cyberbullying Research Center.

“Cyberbullying shares many features with traditional forms of harassment, including a clear intent to harm, and the hostile use of power within the context of a relationship.”

—Marlene Sandstrom, “More Insidious Harassment,” *New York Times*, September 30, 2010. www.nytimes.com.

Sandstrom is professor of psychology at Williams College; her research focuses on social vulnerability during childhood and peer relationships at school.

How Serious a Problem Is Cyberbullying?

- A 2011 survey of teens and young adults by the Associated Press and MTV found that **56 percent** of respondents had been the target of some type of online taunting, harassment, or bullying.

- In a 2010 study of middle school students by Sameer Hinduja and Justin W. Patchin of the Cyberbullying Research Center, nearly **30 percent** of respondents reported being cyberbullied two or more times in the previous 30 days.

- In an October 2010 poll of 1,000 adults by Rasmussen Reports, **69 percent** of respondents said that physical bullying and cyberbullying are equally dangerous.

- According to a November 2010 report by the Bureau of Justice Statistics, of youths aged 12 to 18 who had been cyberbullied, **13 percent** said it occurred once or twice during the school year, **21 percent** said once or twice a month, and **5 percent** said once or twice a week.

- In a study of high school students published in 2010 by Canadian researcher Qing Li, over **70 percent** of participants said that when they witnessed cyberbullying, they watched but did not take part, and **26 percent** who witnessed it chose to get offline rather than watch it.

Texting Most Common Form of Cyberbullying

An August 2011 report by the National Center for Education Statistics found that over 1.5 million students aged 12 to 18 were cyberbullied at or away from school during the 2008–2009 school year, which represents 6 percent of all students. The most common form of cyberbullying involved unwanted text messages, followed by hurtful information posted on the Internet.

Unwanted contact via text messaging	753,000
Hurtful information on Internet	502,000
Unwanted contact via instant messaging	448,000
Unwanted contact via e-mail	335,000
Purposeful exclusion from an online community	224,000
Unwanted contact via online gaming	193,000

Source: National Center for Education Statistics, "Student Reports of Bullying and Cyber-Bullying: Results from the 2009 School Crime Supplement to the National Crime Victimization Survey," August 2011. http:nces.ed.gov.

- A Pew Research Center survey published in November 2011 found that **17 percent** of black teens frequently witnessed mean behavior on social network sites compared with **11 percent** of white teens and **4 percent** of Latino teens.

- A study published in March 2010 by researchers from Iowa State University found that **50 percent** of gay, lesbian, bisexual, or transgender (GLBT) students were regular victims of cyberbullying.

Cyberbullying and Physical Bullying Are Both Dangers

In an October 2010 telephone survey by Rasmussen Reports, 1,000 adults were asked their opinions about bullying and cyberbullying among youth. The majority of respondents thought that both types of bullying were equally dangerous.

Survey participant views on bullying and cyberbullying

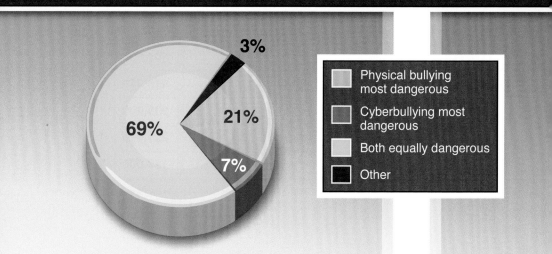

3%

21%

69%

7%

Physical bullying most dangerous

Cyberbullying most dangerous

Both equally dangerous

Other

Source: Rasmussen Reports, "Most Adults Say Physical Bullying, Cyber Bullying Are Equally Dangerous," October 8, 2010. www.rasmussenreports.com.

- In a 2010 survey of teens aged 13 to 17 by the security company McAfee, **14 percent** said they had been involved in some form of cyberbullying behavior, and **22 percent** said they would not know what to do if they were cyberbullied.

- In a study of high school students published in 2010 by Canadian researcher Qing Li, when asked why people cyberbully, **64 percent** of respondents said it was for fun, and **45 percent** thought cyberbullies were mean, bored, and/or having family problems.

Student Experiences with Bullying and Cyberbullying

The most common form of bullying or cyberbullying experienced by students, according to a November 2010 joint report by the Bureau of Justice Statistics and the National Center for Education Statistics, was being made fun of, called names, or insulted. Students who were surveyed also reported other common forms of abuse or harassment including being the subject of rumors and being pushed, tripped, or spit on.

Percentage of students aged 12–18 who reported selected bullying problems at school and cyberbullying problems anywhere during the school year: 2007

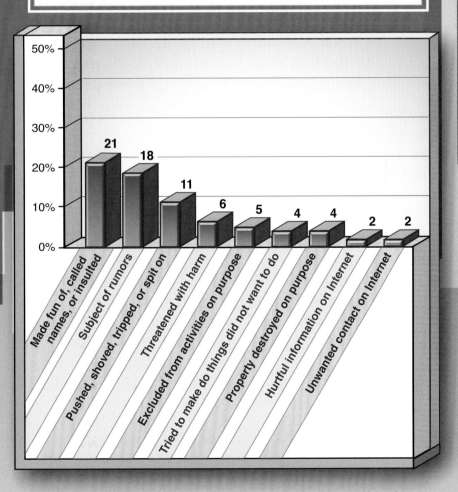

Source: Bureau of Justice Statistics and National Center for Education Statistics, *Indicators of School Crime and Safety: 2010*, November 22, 2010. www.bjs.gov.

What Are the Consequences of Cyberbullying?

66The Internet makes it easy to casually carve up real people in some cartoon world. A drive-by shooting, a stab in the dark. A fast, vicious punch to the reputation. Easy to do damage. And awfully hard to repair.99

—Susan Arnout Smith, a writer from San Diego who was the victim of cyberbullies who created a degrading Facebook profile in her name.

66The effects of cyberbullying are not limited to hurt feelings that can be easily disregarded. The consequences can be far-reaching, and can permanently damage the psyche of many adolescents.99

—Sameer Hinduja and Justin W. Patchin, codirectors of the Cyberbullying Research Center.

In October 2009, when Lynda Lopez was a senior in high school, she learned that she was a finalist for a full-ride scholarship to a small private college in Minnesota. She was thrilled and could not wait to share the exciting news with her friends. So, as she explains, "I did what any teen today would do: I posted it on Facebook."[35] The next day, when Lopez was notified that she was in the running for a different scholarship, she posted about that, too. Like many people who use social networking sites, she had never been concerned about the people she friended or who saw her posts—and little did she know that this would come back to haunt her. "I'd always accepted every friend request," she says, "never thinking it could be dangerous."[36]

A Life Nearly Ruined

Soon after Lopez's posts appeared on Facebook, she was shocked to receive a phone call from a foundation that had offered one of the scholarships. The caller said she had received Lopez's e-mail saying that she "wanted to drop out of the program because the scholarship was a piece of crap."[37] After assuring the woman that she had not sent the e-mail, Lopez had another disturbing phone conversation. A representative from another foundation said that its president was deeply upset over an insulting e-mail from Lopez. Again she explained that the message was not from her and that someone was obviously trying to sabotage her chances at the scholarship. This was upsetting enough—but then Lopez started getting e-mails that accused her of stealing the scholarships. At least one e-mail even threatened her life. At that point, Lopez got scared and contacted the police.

Lopez says that the death threats were not taken seriously by the police department because weeks passed before she heard anything from them. Finally a detective called and, after an investigation, was able to track down the cyberbully. It proved to be a girl who had once worked with Lopez, a disgruntled teenager who was envious after reading about the scholarships on Facebook. The girl was charged with electronic harassment and sentenced to a one-year probation period. Since Lopez could prove that she had nothing to do with the e-mails, her applications went forward and ultimately she was awarded a full scholarship to the University of Chicago. But she learned a tough lesson about privacy settings on social networking sites and the damage cyberbullies can do to unsuspecting people. She writes: "This person could have jeopardized my college education."[38]

> " According to the National Crime Prevention Council, young people who are cyberbullied often feel that they do not have a safe retreat from the abuse, which can cause them a great deal of emotional pain. "

Consumed by Fear and Dread

Most people now know that the online harassment and abuse of cyberbullying can have serious consequences. According to the National Crime Prevention Council, young people who are cyberbullied often feel that they do not have a safe retreat from the abuse, which can cause them a great deal of emotional pain. After relentless taunting by cyberbullies, one 14-year-old girl from New Jersey shared her experience in an e-mail to the Cyberbullying Research Center: "It's torment and hurts. They say 'sticks and stones may break my bones, but words will never hurt me.' That quote is a lie and I don't believe in it. Sticks and stones may cause nasty cuts and scars, but those cuts and scars will heal. Insultive words hurt and sometimes take forever to heal."[39]

In his June 2010 testimony at the hearing on student cyber safety, Phillip C. "Dr. Phil" McGraw talked about the psychological damage that cyberbullying can do to young people, saying that he has personally witnessed their torment. They become depressed and withdrawn, and some develop symptoms of post-traumatic stress disorder—yet most suffer silently because they are too ashamed to tell a parent or other authority figure. McGraw explained: "They become even more humiliated—and yes, more isolated—as the cyber-bullying continues for weeks, months, and even years."[40]

Shattered Self-Esteem

Few studies have focused on the connection between cyberbullying and self-esteem, which is the negative or positive way people view themselves and their self-worth. Extensive research has, however, been published about bullying in general and has revealed that victims tend to have lower self-esteem than those who are not bullied. According to Sameer Hinduja and Justin W. Patchin of the Cyberbullying Research Center, the reasons for this link are not clear: "It may be that the experience of being victimized decreases one's self-esteem, or that those who have low self-esteem are more likely to be targeted as victims."[41]

To examine the effects of cyberbullying on young people's self-esteem, Hinduja and Patchin performed a study in 2010 that involved 2,000 middle school students in one of the largest school districts in the United States. The study revealed that 30 percent of the teens had been victims of cyberbullying at least two times during the past 30 days, and those who were cyberbullied had significantly lower self-esteem than the teens who had not. This finding is significant because low self-esteem has been closely connected with many problems that can have a negative effect on adolescents' health and well-being. In a summary report of the study, Hinduja and Patchin write: "Specifically, previous research has shown a . . . correlation between self-esteem and academic achievement, absenteeism, poor health, criminal behavior, and other problematic consequences."[42]

Cyberbullied and Depressed

Depression is not uncommon among young people who are tormented by cyberbullies. There are numerous reasons for this, including the overwhelming sadness that comes from being abused by their peers and the fact that cyber abuse is nonstop, staring victims in the face whenever they turn on the computer or check their phones for text messages. Says Ronald Iannotti, a researcher with the National Institutes of Health: "Individuals can be more isolated when bullying occurs by cell phone or computer. The mechanism for cyber bullying is 'I'm making fun of you; I could have made a photo of you that's not even true and it can go to Facebook.' The audience is much greater. That can be devastating—not knowing how many people have seen that text message or photo."[43]

In September 2010 Iannotti and his colleagues announced the findings of a study that examined the relationship between cyberbullying and depression in youth. The team analyzed data from a health behavior survey that involved thousands of students in sixth through tenth grade and found that about 14 percent had experienced cyberbullying. The team also determined that the kids who had been cyberbullied had much higher rates of depression than those who had not. In the published study, which

> " Few studies have focused on the connection between cyberbullying and self-esteem, which is the negative or positive way people view themselves and their self-worth. "

appeared in the April 2010 issue of the *Journal of Adolescent Health*, the authors write: "Cyber victims reported higher depression than bullies or bully-victims, a result not observed in other forms of bullying. . . . Results indicated the importance of further study of cyber bullying because its association with depression was distinct from traditional forms of bullying."[44]

Gay Teens at Risk

Research has clearly shown that males and females of all ages and all walks of life have been victimized by cyberbullies. A consistent finding, though, is that gay, lesbian, bisexual, and transgender (GLBT) teens are bullied at much higher rates than straight teens. This was the focus of a study published in March 2010 by researchers from Iowa State University. In an online survey of 444 students from middle school through college, over 50 percent of the GLBT respondents said they had been victims of cyberbullying in the 30 days prior to the survey. Of those, 45 percent reported feeling depressed as a result of being cyberbullied, 38 percent felt embarrassed, and 28 percent felt nervous about attending school. Says Warren Blumenfeld, who was the study's lead researcher: "Especially at this age, this is a time when peer influences are paramount in a young person's life. If one is ostracized and attacked, that can have devastating consequences—not only physically, but on their emotional health for the rest of their lives."[45]

Depression is not uncommon among young people who are tormented by cyberbullies.

One teenager who endured relentless abuse because of his sexual orientation was Jamey Rodemeyer, a 14-year-old boy from Buffalo, New York. As far back as grade school he was taunted by bullies who surrounded him in the hallways, ridiculing him because all his friends were girls and calling him offensive names like "fag" and "faggot." By the time Rodemeyer was in middle school the bullying had become overwhelming, as it was happening not only in person but also online. The cyberbullies made anonymous comments on his Formspring page that he was stupid, fat, and ugly. One post was particularly vicious, saying: "I wouldn't care if you died. No one would.

So just do it :) It would make everyone WAY more happier!"[46]

As agonizing as this abuse was for Rodemeyer, he wanted to do something to help other young people who were suffering like he was. In May 2011, after admitting to his friends that he was bisexual, he posted a YouTube video on the website of the It Gets Better Project, which was created to reassure GLBT youth that life will improve as they get older. In Rodemeyer's video, he said: "Love yourself and you're set. . . . I promise you, it will get better."[47] Four months later, he posted a farewell message on the Tumblr website and then took his own life.

Bullied to Death?

After news spread of Rodemeyer's tragic death, people were outraged, saying that he exemplified the abuse that is inflicted on young people who are bullied. Lady Gaga, a popular singer who was the boy's idol, expressed her sadness and anger on Twitter and dedicated a song to him during a live concert. Numerous others spoke out as well, such as author and nationally syndicated columnist Dan Savage. On September 20, 2011, the day he learned about Rodemeyer's suicide, Savage wrote on his blog: "His tormenters need to be held to account . . . for their actions, for their hate, for the harm they've caused. They should be asked if they're 'WAY more happier' now, if they're pleased with themselves, and if they have anything to say to the mother of the child they succeeded in bullying to death."[48]

> One teenager endured relentless abuse because of his sexual orientation.

Although the idea that someone could be bullied to death is often debated, some psychologists maintain that victims can be so deeply wounded they feel as though life is no longer worth living. Steve Gerali, a psychologist and the author of *What Do I Do When Teenagers Are Depressed and Consider Suicide?* shares his thoughts: "What happens is kids who are cyber-bullied tend to see this as a hopeless situation—no matter where they go, they can't escape it because it's online. So suicide becomes a means to escape it."[49]

Yet as terrible and tragic as suicides are, whether these deaths can be directly attributed to cyberbullying is controversial, with some experts saying that the real issue is mental health problems that were undiagnosed. Their contention is that bullying in any form cannot *cause* suicide, and by pinning the blame on cyberbullying, deeper psychological issues are ignored. Ken Trump, president of National School Safety and Security Services, writes:

> As a parent and as a school safety professional for over 25 years, I don't want to see any parent lose their child. Nor do I have any desire to minimize the urgency, seriousness, or need to address teen suicide. But the conversation clearly must shift to one on teen mental health needs. At best, bullying is one factor in some incidences which might contribute to—but not solely cause—a teen suicide.[50]

Misery, Agony, and Tragedy

People who are cyberbullied suffer from innumerable problems, including constant dread, fear, low self-esteem, and depression. Some, like Lynda Lopez, come close to having their reputations ruined while others, like Jamey Rodemeyer, would rather end their lives than endure the barrage of insults and humiliation one more day. No one knows what the solution is, or even if there is one—but few would disagree that the abuse needs to stop.

What Are the Consequences of Cyberbullying?

❝Technology has the potential to enhance the life and learning of today's youth. When it is misused, it has the power to devastate the victim with consequences that can last a lifetime.❞

> —Jan Urbanski and Steve Permuth, *The Truth About Bullying: What Educators and Parents Must Know and Do.* Lanham, MD: Rowman & Littlefield, 2009, p. 68.

Urbanski supervises the Safe and Drug Free Schools Office in Pinellas County, Florida, and Permuth is professor of education at the University of South Florida.

....

❝Cyberbullying inspires psychological reactions that are very similar to traditional bullying: low self-esteem, frustration, shock, depression, and anxiety are only some of the many consequences, often leaving the victim with long-lasting emotional scars that extend far into adulthood.❞

> —Independent Democratic Conference, *Cyberbullying: A Report on Bullying in a Digital Age*, September 2011. www.nysenate.gov.

The Independent Democratic Conference is composed of four New York state senators who formed their own independent caucus.

....

* Editor's Note: While the definition of a primary source can be narrowly or broadly defined, for the purposes of Compact Research, a primary source consists of: 1) results of original research presented by an organization or researcher; 2) eyewitness accounts of events, personal experience, or work experience; 3) first-person editorials offering pundits' opinions; 4) government officials presenting political plans and/or policies; 5) representatives of organizations presenting testimony or policy.

> **With the click of a button, embarrassing images, sensitive information, or even misinformation can be sent to hundreds, thousands, even millions of people. Once information or an attack is made public on the Internet it can be impossible to remove it, leaving a legacy of the event that can haunt an individual for years.**

—New York State Office of Cyber Security, "Cyber Bullying: What You Need to Know to Keep Your Family Safe," *Cyber Security Tips Newsletter*, May 2011. www.dhses.ny.gov.

The New York State Office of Cyber Security is charged with deterring and responding to cyber crime and promoting cyber security awareness within the state.

> **Many experts confirm that the psychological effects on our children can be as devastating, and may be even more so than traditional bullying.**

—Michele Borba, "9 Signs of Cyberbullying," *Reality Check* (blog), April 7, 2010. www.micheleborba.com.

Borba is a child and adolescent psychologist, educator, and contributor to NBC News.

> **Children who are cyber bullied experience depression, anxiety, low self-esteem, physical health consequences, and poor academic performance.**

—Robin Kowalski, interviewed by Alexandra L. Barzvi, "Social Networking for Tweens and Teens: Cyberbullying," Alexandra L. Barzvi, October 24, 2010. www.drbarzvi.com.

Kowalski is a professor in the Department of Psychology at Clemson University in South Carolina and the author of *Cyberbullying: Bullying in the Digital Age*.

> **Cyberbullying has not existed long enough to have solid research, but there is evidence that it may be an early warning for more violent behavior.**

—United States Computer Emergency Readiness Team (US-CERT), "Dealing with Cyberbullies," June 1, 2011. www.us-cert.gov.

The US-CERT is the operational arm of the US Department of Homeland Security's National Cyber Security Division.

66 Participation in bullying as a victim and/or as a perpetrator is significantly linked to safety risks including running away from home, daily smoking, alcohol and drug abuse, carrying a weapon, school absenteeism, physical fights, self-inflicted or accidental injuries and, above all, suicidal attempts. 99

—Jorge C. Srabstein, testimony before the Council of the District of Columbia, Committee on Libraries, Parks and Recreation, *Bill 19-11: Bullying and Intimidation Act of 2011*, May 2, 2011. www.childrensnational.org.

Srabstein is a psychiatrist and medical director of the Clinic for Health Problems Related to Bullying at Children's National Medical Center.

66 Since cyberbullying occurs in virtual space (and without physical contact), victims can experience the double anguish of being powerless to stop their harassment and unable to prove who's harassing them. 99

—Harold Koplewicz, "The Psychiatric Issues Behind Cyberbullying," *Huffington Post*, July 28, 2010. www.huffingtonpost.com.

Koplewicz is a child and adolescent psychiatrist and president of the Child Mind Institute.

66 Like traditional forms of youth violence, electronic aggression is associated with emotional distress and conduct problems at school. 99

—Centers for Disease Control and Prevention (CDC), "Electronic Aggression," August 30, 2011. www.cdc.gov.

As the premier public health agency in the United States, the CDC conducts and supports a wide array of health-related activities and research.

What Are the Consequences of Cyberbullying?

- A 2009 report by the Centers for Disease Control and Prevention stated that young people who were victims of cyberbullying were more likely than nonvictims to use **alcohol and other drugs**, receive **school detention** or **suspension**, or **skip school**.

- In a survey published in 2011 that involved nearly 400 school social workers, **85.7 percent** either agreed or strongly agreed that cyberbullying could contribute to suicide among students.

- According to a 2011 survey of teens and young adults by the Associated Press and MTV, **14 percent** of respondents who had been cyberbullied had received mental health treatment in the past year, compared with **5 percent** of non-cyberbullying victims.

- In a study of high school students published in 2010 by Canadian researcher Qing Li, when students were asked about the consequences of telling someone they had been cyberbullied, less than **15 percent** said things improved, **5.6 percent** said the cyberbullying got worse, **40 percent** said nothing changed, and the remainder had not told anyone.

- A study published in 2010 by researchers from the National Institutes of Health found that students in grades 6 through 10 who were either perpetrators of cyberbullying or victims had higher levels of **depression** than those not involved in cyberbullying.

Negative Effects of Cyberbullying on Teens

Research has shown that when young people are cyberbullied, it can take a heavy toll on school success and emotional health. In a Pew Research Center survey published in November 2011, nearly 800 teens were asked about their personal experiences on social network sites. This graph shows the problems that were reported.

Have you, personally, ever had an experience on a social network site that . . .

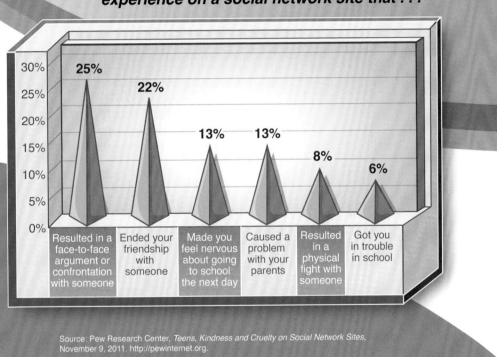

	25%	22%	13%	13%	8%	6%
	Resulted in a face-to-face argument or confrontation with someone	Ended your friendship with someone	Made you feel nervous about going to school the next day	Caused a problem with your parents	Resulted in a physical fight with someone	Got you in trouble in school

Source: Pew Research Center, *Teens, Kindness and Cruelty on Social Network Sites*, November 9, 2011. http://pewinternet.org.

- In a study published in 2010 that involved over 2,200 teenagers from Finland, **1 out of 4** participants who had been cyberbullied said it had made them **fear for their safety**.

- In a 2010 study by researchers from Iowa State University, **45 percent** of the Gay Lesbian Bisexual Transgender (GLBT) teens and young adults who had been cyberbullied became depressed.

Kids Say Telling About Cyberbullying Does Not Help

Parents and educators often encourage young people to tell a trusted adult if they are being cyberbullied, but surveys have shown that most kids keep it to themselves. During a 2010 study by Canadian researcher Qing Li, when high school students were asked whether they had told someone they were being cyberbullied, nearly 40 percent said they had not. Of those who did report the incidents, the majority said that nothing changed, as this graph shows.

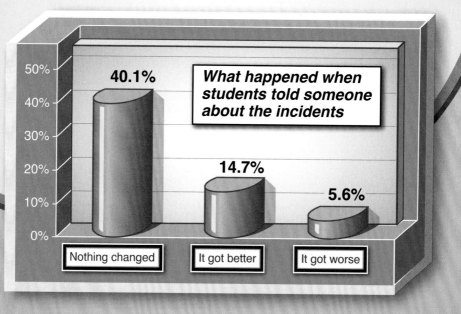

What happened when students told someone about the incidents

- Nothing changed: 40.1%
- It got better: 14.7%
- It got worse: 5.6%

Source: Qing Li, "Cyberbullying in High Schools: A Study of Students' Behaviors and Beliefs About This New Phenomenon," *Journal of Aggression, Maltreatment & Trauma*, 2010. www.tandfonline.com.

- In a 2011 survey of teens and young adults by the Associated Press and MTV, **34 percent** of respondents said they were either very likely or somewhat likely to retaliate against someone who had cyberbullied them.

- According to the Cyberbullying Research Center, cyberbullying victims are nearly two times more likely than nonvictims to have **attempted suicide**.

Cyberbullying and Suicide Risk

Youths who are targeted by cyberbullies are at risk for suicide, according to a 2010 study by the Cyberbullying Research Center. The study surveyed young people between the ages of 10 and 16. It found that 20 percent of respondents who experienced cyberbullying reported seriously thinking about attempting suicide, while 19 percent reported actual suicide attempts. The study also found that cyberbullied males more often thought about and attempted suicide than female targets of cyberbullying.

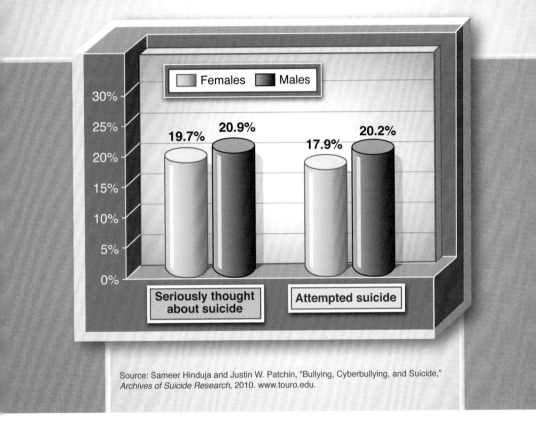

Source: Sameer Hinduja and Justin W. Patchin, "Bullying, Cyberbullying, and Suicide," *Archives of Suicide Research*, 2010. www.touro.edu.

- A study published in March 2010 by researchers from Iowa State University found that more than **one-fourth** of GLBT teens and young adults who had been cyberbullied had suicidal thoughts.

Are More Stringent Cyberbullying Laws Needed?

❝Let's not delude ourselves into thinking that this battle will be won in the legislatures, school board meeting rooms, or courts. We can't legislate compassion or responsibility. And we can't punish kids into being better people.❞

—Rick Phillips, executive director and founder of the youth empowerment and violence prevention group Community Matters.

❝The law must evolve to address how our society communicates, promoting proper conduct, and deterring future bullying with a legal means to punish those who cause harm.❞

—Daniel K. Gelb, a former prosecutor who is now a partner in the Boston law firm Gelb & Gelb.

When he decided to ridicule a teenage boy by exploiting nude photos on the Internet, Matthew Bean had no idea that it would capture the attention of the FBI—or that he would end up in a federal prison because of it. In 2004 the boy had posted sexually explicit photos of himself on 4chan, a website known as an "imageboard" that was designed for posting images. Five years later Bean happened upon the photos, plucked them off the boy's 4chan page, and posted them on his own page. He then invited others to comment on the photos and people eagerly chimed in, forming what prosecutors later called an electronic mob. Together they taunted the boy, with one poster (who Bean insists was not him) writing: "Lets make this kid want to die."[51]

Cyberbullying and Federal Law

After the FBI tracked Bean down and arrested him, prosecutors charged him with 15 felony counts, including the intentional distribution of sexually explicit photos of a minor. For that charge alone Bean was facing five years in prison, so in the hope of receiving a lighter punishment he pleaded guilty to a lesser offense. On January 25, 2011, US district court judge Anita Brody sentenced Bean to 45 days in federal prison, along with five years' probation and $2,000 in fines. He was also ordered to post a message on the 4chan site to let people know that cyberbullying is a crime and that law enforcement officers will pursue it vigorously. After the sentencing, Brody shared her thoughts about the harm caused by cyberbullies: "You have to be blind to what's going on in this world not to know the effect of cyberbullying on present-day society."[52]

The reason Bean was subject to federal rather than state law is because exploiting sexually explicit images of anyone under the age of 18 is a federal offense. If pornography had not been involved, it would undoubtedly have been more challenging for prosecutors to build a case against Bean because cyberbullying itself is not a federal crime. Although various relevant federal laws do exist, these are not applicable to many cyberbullying cases. For example, electronic harassment laws are often

> " Since federal laws do not offer protection for many who are cyberbullied, some people are convinced that a federal cyberbullying law is necessary. "

applicable only if a tangible threat has been made. The federal telephone harassment statute (which also pertains to the Internet) applies only when perpetrators communicate anonymously by using a pseudonym. Also, the law is limited to direct communication between the perpetrator and the victim, so it would not apply to abusive messages posted on a social networking site, blog, or other website.

Since federal laws do not offer protection for many who are cyberbullied, some people are convinced that a federal cyberbullying law is necessary. One supporter of such a law is Linda Sánchez, a US representative from California. In 2009 Sánchez introduced the Megan Meier Cyberbullying Prevention Act, which was named after a 13-year-old Missouri girl who committed suicide after being relentlessly harassed on MySpace. In defense of the bill, Sánchez refers to the various crimes that are currently punishable under federal law, including stalking, sexual harassment, and identity theft. "All of these actions have consequences,"[53] she says, compared with cyberbullying, which is not a violation of federal law. She writes:

> Do we not think it is as serious because it takes place in cyberspace and not face to face? . . . It's happening everywhere and it follows kids home—occurring at any hour of the day or night. Cyberbullying is hurtful enough and affecting kids enough that its victims have turned to suicide or violence just to make it stop. Should we just ignore it? Pass it off as simple child's play?[54]

Although a number of legislators shared Sánchez's passion for the bill, it lacked enough support in the US Congress to become law. Opponents were relieved, as they are strongly convinced that making cyberbullying a federal crime is not the answer to stopping it. One reason for their objection is that the language in such a bill could too easily be misinterpreted by the courts. This, opponents argue, could lead to criminal charges being filed against someone who was merely expressing a controversial opinion on a social networking site or blog. Says UCLA law professor Eugene Volokh: "The [Megan Meier] bill defines [cyberbullying] as 'using electronic means to support severe, repeated and hostile behavior,' but what does 'severe, hostile and repeated behavior' mean? I've written several articles opposing the bill that have appeared online. That's electronic and—because I've written a few of them—repeated. I was also severe and hostile in my criticisms. Under her law, I can now go to jail."[55]

Another Tragedy, Another Proposed Law

The failure of the Megan Meier Cyberbullying Prevention Act did not deter supporters of a federal cyberbullying law from pursuing legislation—and it was another suicide that led to the creation of a different bill. Tyler Clementi was an 18-year-old freshman at Rutgers University. On September 19, 2010, he asked his roommate, Dharun Ravi, if he could have some privacy for a few hours and Ravi agreed—then went to the room of a friend and turned on a webcam that he had secretly installed in the room he shared with Clementi. Ravi filmed Clementi having an intimate encounter with another man and streamed it live on the web, while posting accompanying commentary on Twitter: "I saw him making out with a dude. Yay."[56] When Clementi learned how his privacy had been violated, he was so humiliated and distraught that he wanted to die. After posting a cryptic farewell message on Facebook, he drove to the George Washington Bridge and jumped to his death.

The following November, two US congressmen (Frank Lautenberg and Rush Holt) cosponsored a new cyberbullying bill called the Tyler Clementi Higher Education Anti-Harassment Act. The law would require any college or university that receives federal funding to implement a policy prohibiting harassment of any type based on race, color, national origin, sex, disability, sexual orientation, gender identity, or religion. Schools would be required to acknowledge cyberbullying as a form of harassment, distribute their policies to students, and develop procedures to follow if incidents occur. When the bill was introduced, Lautenberg expressed his thoughts about its importance: "The tragic impact of bullying on college campuses has damaged too many young adults and it is time for our colleges to put policies on the books that would protect students from harassment."[57]

> " The failure of the Megan Meier Cyberbullying Prevention Act did not deter supporters of a federal cyberbullying law from pursuing legislation—and it was another suicide that led to the creation of a different bill. "

Because the proposed law was introduced only a few weeks before the congressional session ended, no action was taken. In March 2011 Lautenberg and Holt reintroduced it for consideration by Congress. As with other proposed cyberbullying laws, this one has been challenged.

One opponent is Greg Lukianoff, who is president of the Foundation for Individual Rights in Education (FIRE). He shares his thoughts: "This bill cannot prevent future students from breaking the law, but it surely will provide students and administrators with new tools to punish views or expression they simply dislike. FIRE's experience demonstrates that when speech is not unambiguously protected, censorship and punishment of unpopular views follows."[58]

States Take Action

In the absence of federal cyberbullying legislation, a number of states have passed their own laws or strengthened laws that already exist. As of November 2011, 35 states had enacted antibullying laws that specifically prohibited electronic harassment and/or cyberbullying. One of these was New Jersey, whose existing legislation was expanded and redesigned in the wake of Clementi's suicide. Within months of his death, New Jersey legislators had crafted the new law, which was signed by the governor in January 2011.

New Jersey's Anti-Bullying Bill of Rights is considered to be some of the toughest antibullying legislation in the United States. It contains procedures for students and school officials to report, investigate, and resolve instances of bullying. It calls for public school employees in the state to complete a training course that includes a component on protecting students from harassment, intimidation, and bullying, including through electronic means. Employees are required to report any bullying incidents of which they become aware, including inside and outside of school. Those who do not comply will face disciplinary action, including the potential loss of their teaching license.

> " In the absence of federal cyberbullying legislation, a number of states have passed their own laws or strengthened laws that already exist. "

Another state that has toughened its stance on cyberbullying is Massachusetts, which passed stringent legislation in 2010. As in New Jersey, the catalyst for the Massachusetts law was teen suicide—specifically, two teens (Carl Joseph Walker-Hoover and Phoebe Prince) who killed themselves in 2009 and 2010, respectively, after being relentlessly bullied and cyberbullied. The Massachusetts law specifically defines the type of bullying that schools must address as not only taking place on school property, or at school-related functions, but also bullying that occurs "at a location, activity, function, or program that is not school-related, or through the use of technology or an electronic device that is not owned, leased, or used by the school district."[59]

Guarding Free Speech

As more states strengthen their laws and US legislators continue to push for a federal cyberbullying law, legal experts warn that such legislation could prove to be unconstitutional. The primary concern is whether it violates the First Amendment, which guarantees freedom of speech. The Constitution does not protect all speech; for example, it is illegal for someone to yell "Fire!" in a crowded theater when there is no fire or to threaten another person's life. But whether cyberbullying is protected speech is a contentious and murky issue. Justin W. Patchin writes: "It can be difficult to hold bullies accountable for their actions (for both adolescents and adults). In a country such as ours that values free speech so highly, many people genuinely believe they can say whatever they want, to whomever they want. We know that is not true, but it isn't clear where exactly the line is."[60]

The issue of cyberbullying being protected speech has been challenged in court on a number of occasions. One case was argued by Los Angeles attorney Evan Cohen, who filed a lawsuit on behalf of his 13-year-old daughter. In May 2008 she got together with some girlfriends at a café and made a video. As she egged them on, the girls bad-mouthed a classmate (known in court papers as "C.C."), using profanity and referring to her as "spoiled," "a brat," "a slut,"[61] and other vulgar terms. That night Cohen's daughter posted the video on YouTube, and she alerted friends that it was online. Upon learning of the video, C.C. was hurt and humiliated and went to the school office with her mother to complain. Cohen's daughter was suspended from school for two days and she took the case to federal court, claiming that her First Amendment rights had been violated.

On November 16, 2009, US district court judge Stephen V. Wilson decided in her favor, saying that the school did not have the right to suspend her. In his ruling, Wilson wrote: "To allow the School to cast this wide a net and suspend a student simply because another student takes offense to their speech, without any evidence that such speech caused a substantial disruption of the school's activities, runs afoul of *Tinker*."[62]

> As more states strengthen their laws and US legislators continue to push for a federal cyberbullying law, legal experts warn that such legislation could prove to be unconstitutional.

Wilson was referring to a Supreme Court decision in the 1969 case *Tinker v. Des Moines Independent Community School District*. In that case, the court ruled that students' rights to free speech could not be infringed upon unless their actions substantially interfered with school operations.

Because cyberbullying has not been addressed by the Supreme Court, lower courts often rely on what has become known as the *Tinker* standard in freedom of speech cases, including cases where cyberbullying was done away from school grounds. According to University of North Carolina law professor Dean Gasaway, the high court will eventually have to address whether schools violate students' free speech rights by punishing them for participating in cyberbullying on their own time, using their own computers. Until that happens, lower courts have no choice but to continue to abide by the *Tinker* standard. Gasaway writes: "Notably, the trend among lower courts appears to allow schools to punish off-campus cyberbullying if such actions cause a material and substantial interference with on-campus school administration."[63]

Questions, Concerns, and Complexities

Few would disagree that cyberbullying is a problem, but whether it should be addressed with tougher laws is controversial. Those who support such efforts say that with the explosive growth of the Internet and digital technology, cyberbullying has gotten out of control, and legislation is the only way to stop it. Others disagree, arguing that new laws could trample people's rights to freedom of speech. As courts are increasingly forced to rule on cyberbullying cases, new questions and controversies are almost certain to arise.

Are More Stringent Cyberbullying Laws Needed?

66 **These hate crimes need to stop. Cyber bullying needs to be a federal crime.** 99

—Elizabeth Lombino, "Suicide of Rutgers Student: Enough Is Enough," Change.org, September 30, 2010. http://news.change.org.

Lombino is a licensed social worker in New York City.

66 **We don't need any new criminal laws. We have more than enough right now—4,000 federal crimes, and many times that number of state crimes.** 99

—Paul Butler, "Not Every Tragedy Should Lead to Prison," *New York Times*, December 3, 2010. www.nytimes.com.

Butler, a former federal prosecutor, is an associate dean and professor of law at George Washington University.

66 We see a place for evidence-based, fiscally supported state legislation that helps clarify school responsibilities and provides them with the tools to better manage bullying and cyberbullying incidents. We haven't seen the perfect law yet. **99**

—Justin W. Patchin, "Another Well-Meaning, but Unfunded Mandate to Address Bullying," Cyberbullying Research Center, September 1, 2011. http://cyberbullying.us.

Patchin is associate professor of criminal justice at the University of Wisconsin–Eau Claire and codirector of the Cyberbullying Research Center.

66 There may be kinks to work out in the new law, but the big picture is that New Jersey is putting itself out in front nationally on the issue of bullying—and standing firmly with the victims. That is the right place to be. **99**

—Adam Cohen, "Why New Jersey's Antibullying Law Should Be a Model for Other States," *Time*, September 6, 2011. http://ideas.time.com.

Cohen is a professor of law at Yale Law School.

66 Prohibiting mean words and cybergossip will never pass constitutional muster. **99**

—Laurie L. Levenson, "What Isn't Known About Suicides," *New York Times*, May 24, 2011. www.nytimes.com.

Levenson is a professor of law at Loyola Law School in Los Angeles, California.

66 In order to preserve the physical and emotional well-being of children and adolescents living and studying in the United States of America, it is critical that the United States Congress should enact Bullying and Cyber-Bullying Prevention Legislation. **99**

—Jorge C. Srabstein, testimony before the Council of the District of Columbia, Committee on Libraries, Parks and Recreation, *Bill 19-11: Bullying and Intimidation Act of 2011*, May 2, 2011. www.childrensnational.org.

Srabstein is a psychiatrist and medical director of the Clinic for Health Problems Related to Bullying at Children's National Medical Center.

66 I don't think we need special cyberbullying laws to protect people from threats that have long been illegal. In addition to the law, schools have the right to intervene if off-campus behavior affects life at school. 99

—Larry Magid, "Time to Take the 'Cyber' Out of Cyberbullying," CNET News, February 3, 2011. http://news.cnet.com.

Magid is a technology journalist, Internet safety advocate, and the founder of the website SafeKids.

66 When so-called free speech leads to bullies having free-rein to threaten kids, it is time to act. 99

—Linda Sánchez, "Protecting Victims, Preserving Freedoms," *Huffington Post*, May 6, 2009. www.huffingtonpost.com.

Sánchez is a US representative from California.

66 Additional criminal penalties would not enhance the needed protection of victims; they merely pile onto current sanctions, regrettably too late to prevent the violation of the rights of those who become targets in an unsafe climate. 99

—Bernard James, "A Human Rights Issue," *New York Times*, September 30, 2010. www.nytimes.com.

James is a professor at Pepperdine University School of Law.

Facts and Illustrations

Are More Stringent Cyberbullying Laws Needed?

- As of November 2011, 35 US states had **antibullying legislation** in place that addressed **electronic harassment**, with 10 of those specifically referring to **cyberbullying**.

- According to data from the Cyberbullying Research Center, over **40 percent** of law enforcement officers surveyed did not know whether their state had a law specific to cyberbullying.

- In an October 2010 poll of 1,000 adults by Rasmussen Reports, **69 percent** of respondents said they thought that cyberbullying should be a punishable crime.

- A BBC poll conducted in June 2009 in the United Kingdom found that **81 percent** of respondents would support a law making cyberbullying a criminal offense.

- In a 2011 survey of teens and young adults by the Associated Press and MTV, **29 percent** of respondents said they had thought about whether things they had posted on a website, Facebook, or MySpace, or shared by text message, would get them in trouble with the police.

- On January 1, 2011, California's first online impersonation law went into effect, which makes digital impersonation punishable with **fines up to $1,000** and/or up to **a year in jail**.

Most Adults Think Cyberbullying Should Be a Crime

Laws about electronic harassment and cyberbullying vary from state to state, with the majority not specifically addressing the issue in legislation. According to an October 2010 survey by Rasmussen Reports, a significant majority of adults think it should be a punishable crime, as this chart shows.

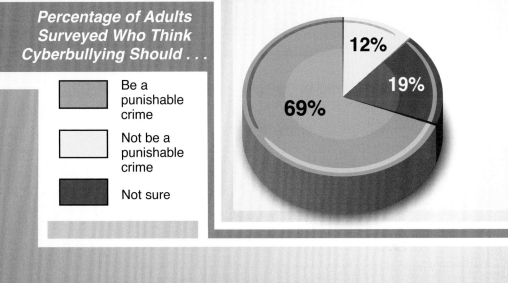

Percentage of Adults Surveyed Who Think Cyberbullying Should . . .

- Be a punishable crime
- Not be a punishable crime
- Not sure

12%

19%

69%

Source: Rasmussen Reports, "Most Adults Say Physical Bullying, Cyber Bullying Are Equally Dangerous," October 8, 2010. www.rasmussenreports.com.

- In a 2011 online poll by the Quincy, Massachusetts, *Patriot Ledger*, **84 percent** of respondents said they thought that criminal charges were justified for cyberbullying cases.

- According to the Cyberbullying Research Center, when police officers were surveyed about cyberbullying, **85 percent** said it was a serious concern that warrants law enforcement attention.

States with Cyberbullying Laws

Nearly all US states have some form of antibullying legislation, and as this map shows, 35 of them address electronic harassment and/or cyberbullying.

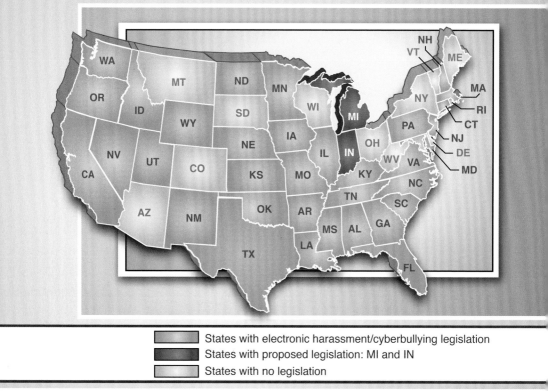

States with electronic harassment/cyberbullying legislation
States with proposed legislation: MI and IN
States with no legislation

Source: Sameer Hinduja and Justin W. Patchin, "State Cyberbullying Laws," Cyberbullying Research Center, November 2011. www.cyberbullying.us.

- In an October 2010 poll of 1,000 adults by Rasmussen Reports, only **5 percent** of respondents believed that police should be responsible for dealing with bullying issues among youth.

- Under North Carolina's 2009 cyberbullying law, considered one of the toughest in the United States, violations are **a criminal offense**, although punishment is less severe for defendants under the age of 18.

Can Cyberbullying Be Prevented?

66 While it's not an epidemic, bullying or just plain mean-
ness is a problem among youth—and adults. I suggest
a national campaign to help stamp it out, just as we've
tried to do with smoking, blatant racism, and sexism
with at least a modicum of success. 99

—Larry Magid, a technology journalist, Internet safety advocate, and the founder of the website SafeKids.

66 Until we agree that cyberbullying is an absolutely un-
acceptable way to treat other people, the cycle of harassment will continue. 99

—Julia Allison, a syndicated columnist and news media expert who has been harassed and threatened by
cyberbullies.

As public awareness of the problem of cyberbullying has grown, this has sparked numerous prevention efforts. After the suicide of Tyler Clementi, Hollywood publicist Jack Ketsoyan became passionate about finding a way to help gay and lesbian bullying victims. "I just kept hearing of these teens committing suicide because they were bullied for being gay," he says, "and my own nephew in New Jersey recently killed himself because he was taunted so heavily because he took a boy to the school dance. I wanted to use my connections here to reach out and help others."[64]

Ketsoyan was aware of a national support project called It Gets Better, which was created in 2010 by syndicated columnist Dan Savage. The purpose of the project is to send a message of hope to gay and lesbian youth that things will get easier for them as time goes by, while at the same time helping to prevent cyberbullying by increasing public awareness. The YouTube channel It Gets Better was created as part of the project, and this gave Ketsoyan the idea of producing a celebrity video by the same name. A host of celebrities including Anne Hathaway, Jenny McCarthy, and Kristin Cavallari, welcomed the chance to be part of Ketsoyan's video, and after it was uploaded to YouTube, other celebrities got involved with their own projects. In his video Neil Patrick Harris urges gay teens to stand tall and be proud of who they are, while Ellen DeGeneres pleads for change in a taped message filmed on the set of her daytime talk show. Among the many popular singers featured in It Gets Better videos are Lady Gaga, Joe Jonas, Adam Lambert, and Ke$ha. As of November 2011 over 20,000 videos had been uploaded to the It Gets Better channel, and the number continues to grow.

> **As public awareness of the problem of cyberbullying has grown, this has sparked numerous prevention efforts.**

Support from the Top

The White House became involved in the fight against bullying and cyberbullying by holding the first Bullying Prevention Summit in March 2011. The event brought together students, teachers, parents, and bullying experts who discussed ways of putting a stop to all forms of bullying. During his opening remarks, President Barack Obama spoke about the purpose of the summit: "If there's one goal of this conference, it's to dispel the myth that bullying is just a harmless rite of passage or an inevitable part of growing up. It's not."[65]

Obama talked about the sobering statistics of bullying among America's youth, and shared his thoughts on the seriousness of cyberbullying in particular: "Today, bullying doesn't even end at the school bell—it can follow our children from the hallways to their cell phones to their computer screens. And in recent months, a series of tragedies has drawn attention to just how devastating bullying can be."[66] To emphasize his commitment to the antibullying fight, Obama appears with his wife,

Michelle, in a video that was posted on Facebook. In the video Obama jokes that he will not bug viewers to make him their Facebook friend, and then gives a more solemn message that bullying is a serious problem that affects every young person in the country.

Facebook Takes Action

In conjunction with the White House's antibullying message, Facebook announced in March 2011 that it would implement changes to promote a culture of respect and help deter cyberbullying. One new addition, called "social reporting," enhances users' ability to report offensive or abusive material. Photos and wall posts can be reported, as can profiles, groups, pages, and events that contain offensive material.

If, for example, users click "Report" on a photo, they are given several options, such as to click either "I don't like this photo" or "This photo is harassing or bullying me." If a user selects the latter, he or she can block the person who posted the photo and/or click a link called "Get help from a trusted friend." This allows the photo to be forwarded, along with a customized message, to someone who can help. In a statement about the new feature, Facebook writes: "Social reporting is a way for people to quickly and easily ask for help from someone they trust. Safety and child psychology experts tell us that online issues are frequently a reflection of what is happening offline. By encouraging people to seek help from friends, we hope that many of these situations can be resolved face to face."[67]

In August 2011 Facebook also announced its Digital Citizenship Research Grants program, which offers $200,000 in grant money for groups to research and create cyberbullying prevention methods. The program is open to nonprofit organizations and educational institutions, and individual grant amounts range from $25,000 to $50,000. After Facebook's announcement, US senator Jay

> " In conjunction with the White House's antibullying message, Facebook announced in March 2011 that it would implement changes to promote a culture of respect and help deter cyberbullying. "

Rockefeller, who chairs the Senate Committee on Commerce, Science, and Transportation, called it an important initiative that is much needed. "I am committed to encouraging kids to harness this technology," says Rockefeller, "but I equally understand the need to expand our understanding of social media and its impact, both positive and negative. This initiative will help us do that."[68]

It Starts with Kids

The National Education Association (NEA) has often spoken out against all forms of bullying and plays a pivotal role in how schools address the problem. The NEA's position is that "one-size-fits-all" bullying prevention programs are not enough because their emphasis is primarily on educators, or what the group calls a top-down approach. Rather, says the NEA, a cultural shift needs to happen, and that involves going directly to students. Lyn Mikel Brown, a college professor and codirector of the group Hardy Girls, Healthy Women, believes that many bullying prevention programs have positive aspects but do not go far enough. "You really have to do this work with students," says Brown. "Those programs don't allow for the messy, on-the-ground work of educating kids. That's what has to happen and it looks different in different schools and communities."[69]

> The notion that young people who are willing to stick up for each other can help curtail bullying has proved to be true in a number of situations.

The NEA emphasizes that young people need to understand how much power they have to help prevent bullying. For instance, if a student sees that someone else is being bullied, he or she has the ability to step up and tell the bully to stop. Although this may not be easy for kids, when peers intervene it can help stop all forms of bullying. This includes cyberbullying, as the NEA writes: "This approach, effective in hallways and cafeterias, also works in online communities, an increasingly common venue for 21st-century bullies. It looks like this: 'I don't think that was very nice what you wrote, and no, I'm not going to forward it to all my friends on Facebook.'"[70]

For any antibullying program to be most effective, says the NEA, prevention efforts need to start when kids are young and just starting to form relationships with other children. This perspective is shared by Meline Kevorkian, the author of *101 Facts About Bullying: What Everyone Should Know*. According to Kevorkian, the earlier kids learn about the dangers of bullying, the more likely it is that prevention measures will be effective. She explains: "The dialogue needs to start in preschool and kindergarten, when these relationships are starting." She adds that in the same way pre-reading skills are taught at an early age, social skills are equally important. For instance, it is critical to reinforce messages such as "If you don't have something nice to say, don't say anything at all."[71] By doing so, seeds can be sown that may help prevent bullying before it starts.

> " The question of whether cyberbullying can be prevented has no easy answers. The problem is serious as well as widespread, and as technology has grown, so has the prevalence of high-tech bullying. "

Teens Helping Teens

The notion that young people who are willing to stick up for each other can help curtail bullying has proved to be true in a number of situations. One teen who has seen this firsthand is Ashley Craig, a 16-year-old high school sophomore from Jefferson Township, New Jersey. After being bullied during middle school and helping a suicidal friend through a difficult time, Craig came up with the idea for a program called Students Against Being Bullied (S.A.B.B.), which she subtitled A New Revolution for a New Generation. She explains: "I had a dream that I could create a program that would help kids fight against bullying. I had the support of family and an army of friends, teachers and administrators, and now we want to spread the message throughout schools in New Jersey and the United States."[72]

Craig's program focuses on four types of bullying: physical, verbal, indirect (such as spreading rumors or ostracizing the victim), and cyberbullying. A key component of S.A.B.B. is support functions such as "report and support lines," whereby students can send a text message to a central school counselor when they witness bullying or are victims of it. Other components include twice-monthly peer support group meetings where students can speak to each other about bullying issues, and interactive presentations that focus on bullying awareness and support. To help students outside of school hours, the report and support lines have access to a hotline where students can send text messages. All communications are kept confidential unless the situation is life threatening. Also, school administrators and teachers are trained in how to handle victims, bystanders, and bullies.

Craig's school has launched the S.A.B.B. program, and she is enthusiastic about the reactions of teachers as well as kids. She explains: "I am very proud of my high school . . . response from the students has been awesome, and I know this program can help stop the terrible problem of bullying."[73] Craig also makes presentations to other schools and hopes eventually to see S.A.B.B. implemented on a larger scale: "I hope to go statewide with this and I will work extremely hard to get there."[74]

High-Tech Solution to a High-Tech Problem

When people talk about ways to prevent cyberbullying, they are usually referring to programs and policies in schools. But Adam Hildreth, who is chief executive officer of the group Crisp Thinking, came up with an idea that can help stop cyberbullying at the moment it occurs—with software designed to monitor it. Hildreth's inspiration came from programs that are designed to screen out spam, as he explains: "I thought hey, if we can stop spam in e-mail why can't we work out what humans are doing to each other online?"[75]

Hildreth's creation is a type of behavioral monitoring software that helps sniff out problem users in online forums such as gaming sites. Built into the program is the unique ability to separate joking from cruelty and to run a sort of "credit check" on the user. Says Hildreth: "What do we know about the user, what are they saying at the moment, and how is the other person [reacting] to what's being said. That doesn't tell us exactly what's going on, but it gives us a great context to make a decision."[76] The program, which is currently in use by Sony Entertainment, the Cartoon Network, and LEGO, gives problematic users one warning before kicking them off the system, and according to Hildreth, its accuracy rate exceeds 98 percent. He says the program offers clients the reassurance "that they can launch new games in environments for kids and teens, every message is being analyzed, and the accuracy of it means that their environment is safe."[77]

Can It Really Get Better?

The question of whether cyberbullying can be prevented has no easy answers. The problem is serious as well as widespread, and as technology has grown, so has the prevalence of high-tech bullying. Yet awareness of the harm caused by cyberbullying has also grown, and this has sparked a surge of prevention efforts, from a White House bullying summit to celebrity videos on YouTube, improved features on social networking sites, and antibullying programs created by teens for teens. Perhaps as more such efforts are launched, fewer people will have to suffer because of the actions of cyberbullies. Psychologist and television host Phillip C. "Dr. Phil" McGraw shares his thoughts: "Times have changed the challenges we face—and we as a society have to change with them. We must change our sensitivities, our policies and our training protocols so we do not let the victims of today's 'keyboard bullies' fall through the cracks."[78]

Can Cyberbullying Be Prevented?

66 No single solution to cyberbullying—or, more properly, bullying in general—exists. There is no one thing that we can do that will protect America's young people from being harmed online. 99

—John Palfrey, testimony before US House of Representatives, Committee on the Judiciary, Subcommittee on Crime, Terrorism, and Homeland Security, Cyberbullying and Other Online Safety Issues for Children: *Hearings on H.R. 1966 and H.R. 3630*, September 30, 2009. http://judiciary.house.gov.

Palfrey is a professor at Harvard Law School and the faculty codirector of the Berkman Center for Internet & Society.

66 As new technology emerges, it is essential to promote safe and responsible use of all types of technology to lessen the devastation that can result from cyberbullying. 99

—Jan Urbanski and Steve Permuth, *The Truth About Bullying: What Educators and Parents Must Know and Do*. Lanham, MD: Rowman & Littlefield, 2009.

Urbanski supervises the Safe and Drug Free Schools Office in Pinellas County, Florida, and Permuth is professor of education at the University of South Florida.

* Editor's Note: While the definition of a primary source can be narrowly or broadly defined, for the purposes of Compact Research, a primary source consists of: 1) results of original research presented by an organization or researcher; 2) eyewitness accounts of events, personal experience, or work experience; 3) first-person editorials offering pundits' opinions; 4) government officials presenting political plans and/or policies; 5) representatives of organizations presenting testimony or policy.

> **If we want to stop cyberbullying, all of the adults who interact with students need to recognize it as something worth stopping.**

—Justin W. Patchin, "Law Enforcement Perspectives on Cyberbullying," Cyberbullying Research Center, September 28, 2011. http://cyberbullying.us.

Patchin is associate professor of criminal justice at the University of Wisconsin–Eau Claire and codirector of the Cyberbullying Research Center.

> **We need more awareness and education into this new world of cyber bullying. The internet provides endless access to so many people and one's privacy can be taken away in an instant. This is a dangerous and scary situation.**

—Elizabeth Lombino, "Suicide of Rutgers Student: Enough Is Enough," Change.org, September 30, 2010. http://news.change.org.

Lombino is a licensed social worker in New York City.

> **We need to give school officials the tools they need to deal with cyber-bullying comprehensively, to address early prevention, early intervention when incidents arise, and chronic situations.**

—Phillip C. McGraw, testimony before US House of Representatives, Committee on Education and the Workforce, Subcommittee on Healthy Families and Communities, "Hearing on Ensuring Student Cyber Safety," June 24, 2010. http://republicans.edlabor.house.gov.

McGraw is a psychologist and the host of the daytime television program *Dr. Phil*.

> **Every adult who interacts with kids—parents, educators, librarians, police, pediatricians, coaches, child care givers—must get educated about this lethal new form of bullying so you can find ways to stop this.**

—Michele Borba, "9 Signs of Cyberbullying," *Reality Check* (blog), April 7, 2010. www.micheleborba.com.

Borba is a child and adolescent psychologist, educator, and contributor to NBC News.

> 66 Cyberbullying can be a complicated issue, especially for adults who are not as familiar with using the Internet, instant messenger, or chat rooms as kids. But like more typical forms of bullying, it can be prevented when kids know how to protect themselves and parents are available to help. 99

—National Crime Prevention Council, "What Is Cyberbullying?," 2011. www.ncpc.org.

The National Crime Prevention Council produces tools that communities can use to learn crime prevention strategies, engage community members, and coordinate with local agencies.

> 66 Antibullying efforts cannot be successful if they make teenagers feel victimized without providing them the support to go from a position of victimization to one of empowerment. 99

—Danah Boyd and Alice Marwick, "Bullying as True Drama," *New York Times*, September 22, 2011. www.nytimes.com.

Boyd is a senior researcher at Microsoft Research and a research assistant professor at New York University, and Marwick is a postdoctoral researcher at Microsoft Research and a research affiliate at Harvard University.

> 66 Just like face-to-face bullying, unfortunately, cyberbullying will always be there. But learning how to deal with it, how to report it and how to protect kids and teens online is a first step in keeping everyone safer online. 99

—Jayne Hitchcock, e-mail interview with author, October 12, 2011.

Hitchcock is an expert on cyberbullying and president of Working to Halt Online Abuse (WHOA) Kids/Teen Division.

Can Cyberbullying Be Prevented?

- In a study released in May 2011 by the National Cyber Security Alliance and Microsoft, over **82 percent** of school administrators and **85 percent** of technology specialists strongly agreed that cybersecurity, cybersafety, and cyberethics should be taught in schools as part of the curriculum.

- In 2009 leaders of the **European Union** signed a pact with Facebook, MySpace, and Google to help protect teenagers who use the sites from cyberbullying.

- According to the National Crime Prevention Council, school anti-cyberbullying policies can be effective because most cyberbullies and **victims know each other from school**.

- In a survey published in 2011 by the American Osteopathic Association, **91 percent** of parents said they, rather than teachers, were ultimately responsible for protecting their children from the effects of cyberbullying.

- In 2009 **Facebook** partnered with five leading Internet safety organizations (Common Sense Media, ConnectSafely, WiredSafety, Childnet International, and The Family Online Safety Institute) to form the Safety Advisory Board.

- In a survey published in 2011 that involved nearly 400 school social workers, the majority of respondents said their schools **did not actively address cyberbullying**.

Educators Not Teaching About Cyberbullying

A May 2011 joint survey by the National Cyber Security Alliance and Microsoft found that 91 percent of teachers believe that Internet ethics, safety, and security issues should be taught as part of a school's curriculum. As this graph shows, however, few teachers are addressing these issues in the classroom.

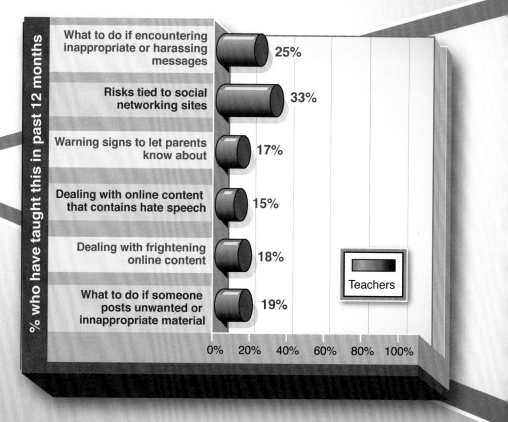

% who have taught this in past 12 months

What to do if encountering inappropriate or harassing messages	25%
Risks tied to social networking sites	33%
Warning signs to let parents know about	17%
Dealing with online content that contains hate speech	15%
Dealing with frightening online content	18%
What to do if someone posts unwanted or innappropriate material	19%

Teachers

0%   20%   40%   60%   80%   100%

Source: National Cyber Security Alliance, "The State of K–12 Cyberethics, Cybersafety and Cybersecurity Curriculum in the United States," May 2011. www.staysafeonline.org.

- In a study released in May 2011 by the National Cyber Security Alliance and Microsoft, **51 percent** of teachers and **81 percent** of administrators believed their school districts were doing an adequate job of preparing students for online safety, security, and ethics.

Kids See Themselves as Key to Stopping Cyberbullying

During a study published in 2010, researchers from Iowa State University asked students who is most responsible for putting a stop to cyberbullying. Most said their peers should do more to stop it, while the fewest number thought it was up to federal or state governments.

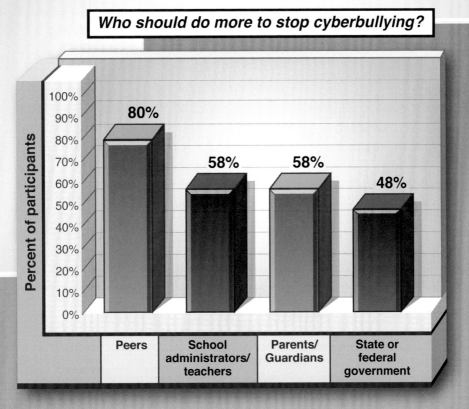

Who should do more to stop cyberbullying?

Percent of participants

- Peers — 80%
- School administrators/teachers — 58%
- Parents/Guardians — 58%
- State or federal government — 48%

Note: Total exceeds 100 percent because participants could give more than one answer.

Source: Warren J. Blumenfeld and R.M. Cooper, "LGBT and Allied Youth Responses to Cyberbullying: Policy Implications," *International Journal of Critical Pedagogy*, March 2010.

- In an October 2010 survey by Care.com, **20 percent** of parents who participated said they would give their schools a grade of **D or F in efforts to educate students** about the dangers of bullying.

Social Workers Address Cyberbullying

From a study published in January 2011, Temple University researchers Karen Slovak and Jonathan B. Singer compiled feedback from nearly 400 school social workers who shared their thoughts about cyberbullying. A large majority see themselves as central to helping students prevent and respond to cyberbullying, but only about half feel confident that they know how to deal with it.

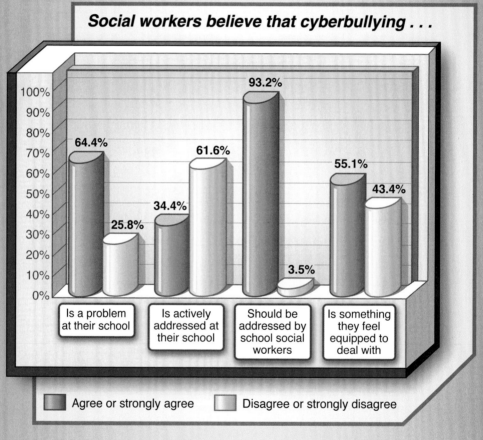

Social workers believe that cyberbullying . . .

	Agree or strongly agree	Disagree or strongly disagree
Is a problem at their school	64.4%	25.8%
Is actively addressed at their school	34.4%	61.6%
Should be addressed by school social workers	93.2%	3.5%
Is something they feel equipped to deal with	55.1%	43.4%

Source: Karen Slovak and Jonathan B. Singer, "School Social Workers' Perceptions of Cyberbullying," *Children & Schools*, January 2011, pp. 5–15.

- In a survey published in 2011 that involved nearly 400 school social workers, **62 percent** of respondents whose schools had cyberbullying policies said the policies were effective.

- An October 2010 survey by Care.com found that **68 percent** of parents were attempting to prevent their children from engaging in cyberbullying by talking to them about it, as well as monitoring their cell phone text messages and social network pages.

- A study released in May 2011 by the National Cyber Security Alliance and Microsoft showed that only **15 percent** of teachers taught students about online hate speech; **18 percent** taught them how to deal with alarming posts, videos, or other web content; and just **26 percent** taught kids how to handle incidents of cyberbullying.

- In an October 2010 survey by Care.com, about **30 percent** of parent respondents had encouraged their schools to create antibullying programs.

Key People and Advocacy Groups

Parry Aftab: An attorney, cyberbullying expert, and activist on behalf of protecting young people from the dangers of cyberspace who founded the group WiredSafety.

Bill Belsey: A Canadian educator and activist, Belsey created the websites bullying.org and cyberbullying.ca and is believed to have coined the term "cyberbullying."

Danah Boyd: A researcher at Microsoft Research and a fellow at Harvard's Berkman Center for Internet and Society who has written extensively on the topics of online social networking and cyberbullying.

Center for Democracy and Technology: A civil liberties group that works to keep the Internet open and available to all, and has spoken out against federal cyberbullying legislation.

Electronic Frontier Foundation: A civil liberties organization that advocates on behalf of the public interest with regard to Internet-related issues such as free speech, privacy, innovation, and consumer rights.

Electronic Privacy Information Center: A public interest research center that seeks to focus public attention on civil liberties issues and to protect privacy, the First Amendment, and constitutional rights.

Sameer Hinduja: An associate professor in the School of Criminology and Criminal Justice at Florida Atlantic University and codirector of the Cyberbullying Research Center.

Jayne Hitchcock: A cyberbullying expert and president of Working to Halt Online Abuse (WHOA) Kids/Teen Division.

Larry Magid: A technology journalist, Internet safety advocate, and the founder of the website SafeKids.

Megan Meier: A 13-year-old Missouri girl who committed suicide after being repeatedly bullied online by a woman posing as a teenage boy. Meier's death led to a proposed cyberbullying law named after her.

Justin W. Patchin: An associate professor of criminal justice at the University of Wisconsin–Eau Claire, codirector of the Cyberbullying Research Center, and a noted authority on cyberbullying.

Linda Sánchez: A US representative from California who introduced legislation that would make it a federal crime for electronic speech that harasses, intimidates, or causes substantial emotional distress to a person.

Debbie Wasserman Schultz: A US representative from Florida who introduced the Adolescent Web Awareness Requires Education Act, which seeks to prevent and reduce cyberbullying through research and education rather than make it a criminal offense.

WiredSafety: A group that provides help, information, and education with the goal of making the Internet safer for everyone.

Chronology

1969
In *Tinker v. Des Moines Independent Community School District*, the US Supreme Court upholds the free speech rights of students if their actions do not cause substantial disruption of or interference with school activities. Years later, lower courts rely on the *Tinker* standard for rulings on cyberbullying cases.

1997
The US Supreme Court affirms a lower court ruling that the Communications Decency Act is unconstitutional because it violates the First Amendment's guarantee of free speech.

1995
CyberAngels is launched on the online chat system Internet Relay Chat and becomes the first Internet-based cyberstalking help program.

1970   **1990**   **1995**

1991
Swiss computer expert Tim Berners-Lee announces his creation of software and a point-and-click browser, thus launching the World Wide Web.

1996
The US Congress passes the Communications Decency Act, which is designed to protect minors from sexually graphic material transmitted through the Internet.

1998
The organization i-SAFE is founded with the goal of educating youth about Internet safety.

1999
US attorney general Janet Reno recommends that cyberstalking be added to existing federal and state stalking laws. The same year, California becomes the first state to pass a law that prohibits cyberstalking.

2000

A federal law that prohibits interstate stalking (physically crossing state lines) is amended to add stalking using e-mail and the Internet.

2010

Two US congressmen introduce legislation called the Tyler Clementi Higher Education Anti-Harassment Act, which would require all public colleges and universities to establish policies that prohibit harassment of students based on race, national origin, gender, disability, sexual orientation, or religion.

2006

President George W. Bush signs Section 113 of the Violence Against Women Act into law. The statute bans people from anonymously using a telephone or a telecommunications device (including the Internet) to annoy, abuse, threaten, or harass any person.

2000   **2005**   **2010**

2003

Ryan Halligan, a 13-year-old boy from Essex Junction, Vermont, commits suicide after years of being bullied in person and online. His father begins to lobby for state laws that address bullying.

2009

US Representative Linda Sánchez introduces the Megan Meier Cyberbullying Prevention Act, which would make electronic speech that harasses, intimidates, or causes substantial emotional distress to a person a federal crime.

2007

The Advertising Council, National Crime Prevention Council, US Department of Justice, and Crime Prevention Coalition of America announce the launch of a joint public service campaign designed to educate preteens and teenagers about how they can help end cyberbullying.

2011

To show its commitment to the problem of bullying and cyberbullying, the White House holds an antibullying summit in Washington, DC.

Related Organizations

Center for Democracy and Technology (CDT)

1634 I St. NW, #1100
Washington, DC 20006
phone: (202) 637-9800 • fax: (202) 637-0968
website: www.cdt.org

The CDT is a civil liberties group that works to keep the Internet open and available to all. Its website features news articles, information on issues such as free expression and online child safety, and a search engine that produces a number of articles on cyberbullying.

Community Matters

652 Petaluma Ave., Suite J-1
PO Box 14816
Santa Rosa, CA 95402
phone: (707) 823-6159 • fax: (707) 823-3373
e-mail: team@community-matters.org
website: www.community-matters.org

Community Matters collaborates with schools and communities to empower youth and help prevent violence. Its website features news articles, video clips, research information, a link to a blog, and a comprehensive section titled "How to Stop School Bullying and Violence."

ConnectSafely

e-mail: admin@connectsafely.org • website: www.connectsafely.org

ConnectSafely is an interactive online-only resource for parents, teens, educators, and others who are interested in Internet safety. The site offers fact sheets, press releases, safety tips, guest commentaries, an online forum, and a search engine that produces numerous articles about cyberbullying.

Cyberbullying Research Center

e-mail: info@cyberbullying.us • website: www.cyberbullying.us

The Cyberbullying Research Center provides information about the nature, extent, causes, and consequences of cyberbullying among adolescents. A wide variety of fact sheets and articles can be accessed through its website.

Family Online Safety Institute (FOSI)

624 Ninth St. NW, Suite 222
Washington, DC 20001
phone: (202) 572-6252
e-mail: fosi@fosi.org • website: http://fosi.org

The FOSI develops public policy, technology, education, and special events pertaining to the online world. Its website features press releases, archived news articles, safety publications for kids and parents, reports on issues such as cyberbullying and sexting, and the *Insight* newsletter.

International Network Against Cyberhate (INACH)

Camperstraat 3 hs
1091 AD Amsterdam, Netherlands
phone: 31-20-6927266 • fax: 31-20-6927267
e-mail: secretariat@inach.net • website: www.inach.net

INACH's mission is to promote respect, responsibility, and citizenship on the Internet through countering cyber-hate and by raising awareness about online discrimination. Its website features reports by INACH and its members, archived news releases, legislation, and video clips.

National Crime Prevention Council

2001 Jefferson Davis Hwy., Suite 901
Arlington, VA 22202-4801
phone: (202) 466-6272 • fax: (202) 296-1356
website: www.ncpc.org

The National Crime Prevention Council produces tools that communities can use to learn crime prevention strategies, engage community members, and coordinate with local agencies. Its website features numerous articles on cyberbullying related to trends, tips for teens, awareness campaigns, and prevention.

National Cyber Security Alliance (NCSA)

1010 Vermont Ave. NW, Suite 821
Washington, DC 20005
phone: (202) 756-2278
e-mail: info@staysafeonline.org • website: www.staysafeonline.org

The NCSA's mission is to educate and empower the public to use the Internet safely and securely at home, work, and school. Its website offers security and safety reports, studies, surveys, fact sheets, a "Safe and Secure Practices" section, and a search engine that produces a number of cyberbullying articles.

Pacer's National Bullying Prevention Center

8161 Normandale Blvd.
Bloomington, MN 55437
phone: (952) 838-9000
website: www.pacer.org/bullying

Pacer's National Bullying Prevention Center seeks to unite, engage, and educate communities to address bullying by providing them with digital resources. Its website offers information, kids' stories about bullying experiences, educational activities, and links to the sister sites TeensAgainstBullying and KidsAgainstBullying.

StopBullying

website: www.stopbullying.gov

StopBullying provides information from various government agencies on how young people, parents, educators, and others in the community can prevent and/or stop bullying. The site features news articles, a "Special Topics" section, and separate areas designed for kids, teens, and young adults.

WiredSafety

c/o IMPS
1 Bridge St., Suite 56
Irvington-on-Hudson, NY 10533
e-mail: info@wiredsafety.org • website: www.wiredsafety.org

WiredSafety seeks to make the Internet safer for everyone and empower them to use the digital technologies responsibly and effectively. Its website offers a vast amount of information related to cyberbullying and links to the sister sites WiredSafety's Teenangels, Tweenangels, Wired-Kids, CyberLawEnforcement, and StopCyberbullying.

For Further Research

Books

Lorna Blumen, *Bullying Epidemic: Not Just Child's Play*. Toronto: Camberley, 2010.

Naomi Drew, *No Kidding About Bullying*. Minneapolis: Free Spirit, 2010.

Lauri S. Friedman, ed., *Cyberbullying*. Farmington Hills, MI: Greenhaven, 2011.

Thomas A. Jacobs, *Teen Cyberbullying Investigated: Where Do Your Rights End and Consequences Begin?* Minneapolis: Free Spirit, 2010.

Robyn MacEachern and Geraldine Charette, *Cyberbullying: Deal with It and Ctrl Alt Delete It*. Toronto: Lorimer, 2011.

Samuel C. McQuade, Sarah Gentry, and Nathan Fisk, *Cyberbullying and Cyberstalking*. New York: Chelsea House, 2011.

Peter Ryan, *Online Bullying*. New York: Rosen, 2010.

Periodicals

Adam Cohen, "New Jersey Enacts Nation's Toughest Law on Bullying," *Time*, September 6, 2011.

Holly C. Corbett, "[Delete] Digital Drama: Words Do Hurt. They Can Even Kill," *Seventeen*, August 2011.

Current Events, "Your Space: Schools Struggle to Find Ways to Curb Cyberbullying Without Violating Student Rights," October 25, 2010.

Michelle R. Davis, "Schools Tackle Legal Twists and Turns of Cyberbullying," *Education Week*, February 9, 2011.

John C. Dvorak, "The Cyberbully Bugaboo," *PC Magazine*, October 20, 2010.

Megan Feldman, "Why Are Nice, Normal Girls Getting Bullied Online?," *Glamour*, March 2010.

Miguel Helft, "Facebook Wrestles with Free Speech and Civility," *New York Times*, December 12, 2010.

Jason Koebler, "Cyber Bullying Growing More Malicious, Experts Say," *U.S. News & World Report*, June 3, 2011.

Lynda Lopez, "How a Cyberbully Almost Ruined My Life, *New York Times Upfront*, September 6, 2010.

Apryl Lundsten, "Attacked Online," *Girls' Life*, August/September 2010.

Weekly Reader News Edition, "Bully Bust! State Lawmakers Get Tough with Cyberbullies," September 2, 2011.

Kathy Wilmore, "Cyberbullying: Technology Is Making Bullying Easier to Do, and Harder to Escape," *Junior Scholastic*, November 22, 2010.

Sarah Zay, "What Sticks & Stones Can't Do, Facebook Will—and More!," *USA Today* magazine, March 2011.

Internet Sources

Ganda At, "Should Schools Punish Cyberbullies?," CNN, October 7, 2010. www.cnn.com/2010/LIVING/10/06/p.schools.punish.cyber bullies/index.html?iref=allsearch.

Emily Bazelon, "How Should Facebook and MySpace Handle Cyberbullying?," *Slate*, March 25, 2010. www.slate.com/id/2248764.

Mary Ellen Flannery, "Does Bullying Really Get Better?," NEA Today, January 19, 2011. http://neatoday.org/2011/01/19/does-bullying -really-get-better.

Jan Hoffman, "A Girl's Nude Photo, and Altered Lives," *New York Times*, March 26, 2011. www.nytimes.com/2011/03/27/us/27sexting.html? _r=1&pagewanted=all.

Larry Magid, "Time to Take the 'Cyber' Out of Cyberbullying," CNet, February 3, 2011. http://news.cnet.com/8301-19518_3-20030511 -238.html.

Joy Resmovits, "Erasing Cyberbullying, One Keystroke at a Time," *Huffington Post*, May 6, 2011. www.huffingtonpost.com/2011/05/06/ cyberbullying-students-erase_n_858832.html.

Susan Arnout Smith, "The Fake Facebook Profile I Could Not Get Removed," *Salon*, February 1, 2011. www.salon.com/2011/02/02/my _fake_facebook_profile.

Source Notes

Overview

1. Quoted in Brian Messenger, "Cyberbullying Latest Challenge for Teen Cancer Survivor," video, *North Andover (MA) Eagle-Tribune*, April 17, 2011. www.eagletribune.com.
2. Marie Hartwell-Walker, "Cyberbullying and Teen Suicide," Psych Central, February 2010. http://psychcentral.com.
3. Quoted in Federal Bureau of Investigation, "New Jersey Man Sentenced for Cyberstalking," January 18, 2011. www.fbi.gov.
4. Quoted in Sameer Hinduja and Justin W. Patchin, "Cyberbullying: Identification, Prevention, and Response," Cyberbullying Research Center, 2010. www.cyberbullying.us.
5. Millie Anne Cavanaugh, "Cyberbullying Can Have Deadly Consequences," Aspen Education Group, 2009. www.aspeneducation.com.
6. Nancy Willard, "Educator's Guide to Cyberbullying, Cyberthreats & Sexting," Center for Safe and Responsible Use of the Internet, April 2007. http://csrui.org.
7. Quoted in Chris Webster, "David Knight," Cyberbullying Info, September 2011. www.cyberbullying.info.
8. Quoted in Stephanie Chen, "In a Wired World, Children Unable to Escape Cyberbullying," CNN, October 4, 2010. http://articles.cnn.com.
9. Olweus Bullying Prevention Program, "What Is Cyber Bullying?," 2011. www.olweus.org.
10. Arthur Kosieradzki, "Know the Warning Signs of Cyberbullying," *Burnsville (MN) Sun Current*, September 14, 2011. www.knowyourrights.com.
11. Parry Aftab, "Why Do Kids Cyberbully Each Other?," STOP Cyberbullying, 2011. www.stopcyberbullying.org.
12. Quoted in Kris Varjas, Jasmaine Talley, Joel Meyers, Leandra Parris, and Hayley Cutts, "High School Students' Perceptions of Motivations for Cyberbullying: An Exploratory Study," *Western Journal of Emergency Medicine*, August 2010. www.ncbi.nlm.nih.gov.
13. Quoted in *Decatur (IL) Herald-Review*, "Cyberbullying Takes Hurt to a New Level," May 9, 2011. www.herald-review.com.
14. Quoted in Mary Ellen Godin, "One Girl's Struggle with Cyber Bullying," *Meriden (CT) Record Journal*, July 18, 2011. www.myrecordjournal.com.
15. Hartwell-Walker, "Cyberbullying and Teen Suicide."
16. Paul Butler, "Not Every Tragedy Should Lead to Prison," Room for Debate, *New York Times*, September 30, 2010. www.nytimes.com.
17. Independent Democratic Conference, *Cyberbullying: A Report on Bullying in a Digital Age*, September 2011. www.nysenate.gov.
18. Aftab, "What Role Does Education and Awareness Play in Addressing Cyberbullying?," Aftab.com. http://aftab.com.
19. Rick Phillips, "Cyberbullying and E-Harassment—a Strategy for Stopping the Epidemic," Common Classroom, February 28, 2011. www.commonsense.com.

How Serious a Problem Is Cyberbullying?

20. Phillip C. McGraw, testimony before US House of Representatives, Committee on Education and the Work-

force, Subcommittee on Healthy Families and Communities, "Hearing on Ensuring Student Cyber Safety," June 24, 2010. http://republicans.edlabor.house.gov.

21. Quoted in AllBusiness, "Cyber-Bullying on Increase, Say Experts," 2010. www.allbusiness.com.

22. Quoted in Rick Nauert, "Virtual Harassment Worse than Face-to-Face," PsychCentral, August 8, 2011. http://psychcentral.com.

23. Quoted in Chen, "In a Wired World, Children Unable to Escape Cyberbullying."

24. Quoted in James Queally, "Newark Teen's Online Identity Stolen and Used to Destroy Her Reputation," Newark (NJ) Star-Ledger, February 13, 2011. www.nj.com.

25. Justin W. Patchin, "Advice for Adult Victims of Cyberbullying," Cyberbullying Research Center blog. November 9, 2010. http://cyberbullying.us.

26. Julia Allison, "Cyberbullying Isn't Just for Kids," Milford (MA) Daily News, March 27, 2011. www.milforddailynews.com.

27. Allison, "Cyberbullying Isn't Just for Kids."

28. Allison, "Cyberbullying Isn't Just for Kids."

29. Susan Arnout Smith, "The Fake Facebook Profile I Could Not Get Removed," Salon, February 1, 2011. www.salon.com.

30. Smith, "The Fake Facebook Profile I Could Not Get Removed."

31. Smith, "The Fake Facebook Profile I Could Not Get Removed."

32. Elizabeth C. Eraker, "Stemming Sexting: Sensible Legal Approaches to Teenagers' Exchange of Self-Produced Pornography," Berkeley Technology Law Journal Annual Review, October 10, 2010. www.btlj.org.

33. Quoted in Jan Hoffman, "A Girl's Nude Photo, and Altered Lives," New York Times, March 26, 2011. www.nytimes.com.

34. Parry Aftab, interviewed by Bonnie Bracey Sutton, "Cyberbullying: An Interview with Parry Aftab," Educational Technology & Change, February 17, 2011. http://etcjournal.com.

What Are the Consequences of Cyberbullying?

35. Lynda Lopez, "How a Cyberbully Almost Ruined My Life," New York Times Upfront, September 6, 2010. http://teacher.scholastic.com.

36. Lopez, "How a Cyberbully Almost Ruined My Life."

37. Lopez, "How a Cyberbully Almost Ruined My Life."

38. Lopez, "How a Cyberbully Almost Ruined My Life."

39. Anonymous, "Share Your Story," Cyberbullying Research Center, 2011. www.cyberbullying.us.

40. McGraw, testimony.

41. Sameer Hinduja and Justin W. Patchin, "Cyberbullying Research Summary: Cyberbullying and Self-Esteem," Cyberbullying Research Center, 2010. www.cyberbullying.us.

42. Hinduja and Patchin, "Cyberbullying Research Summary: Cyberbullying and Self-Esteem."

43. Quoted in Science Daily, "In Cyber Bullying, Depression Hits Victims Hardest," September 26, 2010. www.sciencedaily.com.

44. Jing Wang, Tonja R. Nansel, and Ronald J. Iannotti, "Cyber Bullying and Traditional Bullying: Differential Association with Depression," Journal of Adolescent Health, April 2010. www.cfah.org.

45. Quoted in Live Science, "Cyberbullying Rampant for Lesbian and Gay

Teens," March 10, 2010. www.live science.com.

46. Quoted in Jeannette Torres, "Gay Buffalo Teen Commits Suicide on Eve of National Bullying Summit," Akron News Now, September 22, 2011. www.akronnewsnow.com.

47. Jamey Rodemeyer, YouTube video, May 4, 2011. www.youtube.com.

48. Dan Savage, "Bullied Teenager in Buffalo, NY, Takes His Own Life," *Stranger*, September 20, 2011. http://slog.thestranger.com.

49. Steve Gerali, interviewed by R.J. Carter, "Interview: Dr. Steve Gerali: To Save a Life," The Trades, September 10, 2010. www.the-trades.com.

50. Ken Trump, "Why Teen Mental Health, Not Bullying, Must Be Suicide Focus," *School Security Blog*, September 21, 2010. www.schoolsecurity blog.com.

Are More Stringent Cyberbullying Laws Needed?

51. Quoted in Maryclaire Dale, "NJ Cyberbully Forwarded Lewd Photos, Gets 45 Days," *Business Week*, January 18, 2011. www.businessweek.com.

52. Quoted in Dale, "NJ Cyberbully Forwarded Lewd Photos, Gets 45 Days."

53. Linda Sánchez, "Protecting Victims, Preserving Freedoms," *Huffington Post*, May 6, 2009. www.huffingtonpost .com.

54. Sánchez, "Protecting Victims, Preserving Freedoms."

55. Quoted in Steven Kotler, "Cyberbullying Bill Could Ensnare Free Speech Rights," Fox News, May 14, 2009. www.foxnews.com.

56. Quoted in Lisa W. Foderaro, "Private Moment Made Public, Then a Fatal Jump," *New York Times*, September 29, 2010. www.nytimes.com.

57. Quoted in Kelly Heyboer, "Higher Education Anti-Bullying Bill Is Presented to U.S. House, Senate in Memory of Tyler Clementi," NJ.com, November 18, 2010. www.nj.com.

58. Quoted in Foundation for Individual Rights in Education, "'Tyler Clementi Higher Education Anti-Harassment Act' Threatens Free Speech on Campus," November 23, 2010. http://the fire.org.

59. Quoted in Olweus, "State and Federal Bullying Information: Massachusetts," August 25, 2010. http://olweus.org.

60. Patchin, "Advice for Adult Victims of Cyberbullying."

61. Quoted in Stephen V. Wilson, *J.C., a Minor by and Through Her Guardian ad Litem R.C. v. Beverly Hills Unified School District*, November 16, 2009. http://lawyersusaonline.com.

62. Wilson, *J.C., a Minor by and Through Her Guardian ad Litem R.C. v. Beverly Hills Unified School District*.

63. Dean Gasaway, "Lower Courts, Student Speech, & Cyberbullying," May 2010. www.unc.edu.

Can Cyberbullying Be Prevented?

64. Quoted in Hollie McKay, "Celebrities Share Experiences with Bullies in Wake of Teen Suicides," Fox News, October 7, 2010. www.foxnews.com.

65. Barack Obama, "President Obama and the First Lady at the White House Conference on Bullying Prevention," White House blog, March 10, 2011. www.whitehouse.gov.

66. Obama, "President Obama and the First Lady at the White House Conference on Bullying Prevention."

67. Facebook, "Details on Social Reporting," March 10, 2011. www.facebook .com.

68. Quoted in Kerry Butters, "Facebook to Offer Research Funding," Tech-

Watch, August 3, 2011. www.tech
watch.co.uk.

69. Quoted in Mary Ellen Flannery, "Bullying: Does It Get Better?," National
Education Association, December
2010. www.nea.org.

70. Flannery, "Bullying: Does It Get
Better?"

71. Quoted in Flannery, "Bullying: Does
It Get Better?"

72. Quoted in John R. Luciano, "Freshman Presents Anti-Bullying Program
in Jefferson," NorthJersey.com, May
19, 2011. www.northjersey.com.

73. Quoted in Luciano, "Freshman
Presents Anti-Bullying Program in
Jefferson."

74. Quoted in CBS New York, "NJ Teen
Launches Anti-Bullying Program,"
January 27, 2011. http://newyork.cbs
local.com.

75. Quoted in Joshua Philipp, "Cyberbullying Meets Its Match with Crisp
Thinking," *Epoch Times*, March 28,
2011. www.theepochtimes.com.

76. Quoted in Philipp, "Cyberbullying Meets Its Match with Crisp
Thinking."

77. Quoted in Philipp, "Cyberbullying Meets Its Match with Crisp
Thinking."

78. McGraw, testimony.

List of Illustrations

List of Illustrations

Index

Note: Boldface page numbers indicate illustrations.

Index

About the Author

Peggy J. Parks holds a bachelor of science degree from Aquinas College in Grand Rapids, Michigan, where she graduated magna cum laude. An author who has written over 100 educational books for children and young adults, Parks lives in Muskegon, Michigan, a town that she says inspires her writing because of its location on the shores of Lake Michigan.